"Michelle's work on the importance of connection is so timely. All of us who work in leadership have found that focusing on perfecting a task rather than building relationships creates stress, negativity, and resentment. Today's leaders, both men and women, need to connect with authenticity and compassion to succeed in a chaotic and uncertain time."

—SALLY HELGESEN
Author of *How Women Rise; The Female Advantage;* and *The Web of Inclusion*

"What sets *The Seismic Shift in Leadership: How to Thrive in a New Era of Connection* apart from so many leadership books I have read is the profound clarity and focus of the message and the simplicity of the tools that Michelle provides to reinforce this message throughout the book. The theme of connection with self and others could not be more timely given the challenges our modern society and many of our organizations are facing with so much strife, friction, and discord. Michelle's voice throughout the book is not only instructively clear but also immensely authentic, compassionate, and courageous. And when I got to the end and read the powerful words in her afterword, I had two prevailing thoughts: 1) I wish this book had been written forty years ago when I was a young man filled with so much insecurity about being discovered as a big imposter, and 2) I am so glad I read this amazing book now, as I feel inspired and excited to put Michelle's wisdom into practice in deepening my connections with myself and others in more profound ways."

—GREG HIEBERT
Managing partner, LeadershipForward
Amazon bestselling author, *You Can't Give What You Don't Have: Creating the Seven Habits that Make a Remarkable Life*

"We are in a new era that requires leaders to be authentically connected with themselves, their teams, and their organizations. If you want meaningful results, you need meaningful connection. You can't just focus on results at all costs. We need to focus on creating a value for others that can be done only in productive collaboration. We need to focus on human connection. This book shows us how."

—DR. OLEG KONOVALOV
Thinkers50
Author of *The Vision Code: The da Vinci of Visionary Leadership*

"Michelle Johnston reveals the critical success factor of today's exceptional leaders, namely the power of connection. While it may sound easy, leadership can be a lonely journey at times, and on the human level an authentic connection is harder to experience than we think— and still rare to observe in leadership. Yet, as Michelle's research identifies, employees, peers, and clients seek, first and foremost, trust-based relationships, and they admire people who are "real." That's where this book excels! Its highly relatable stories, practical examples, and reflective questions make it a must-read for anyone wishing to deepen their connection with self and others and to shift their leadership impact to another level."

—ALEX LAZARUS, MSC
Founder, Lazarus and Maverick Limited
Author, *Leading with Influence*
C-suite executive and leadership coach
Keynote speaker

"We are in a new era of disruption which requires leaders to be authentically connected with themselves, their teams, and their organizations. Read this book if you want to learn how to lead more successfully in this new era."

—CHARLENE LI
Founder, Altimeter
New York Times bestselling author, *The Disruption Mindset*

"We are living through unprecedented times that are calling upon all leaders to show up with authenticity, act with intention, and demonstrate the capacity to build relationships. Connection has replaced power as the currency of success. To lead in these challenging times, you must understand the strategies required to leverage it. *The Seismic Shift in Leadership: How to Thrive in a New Era of Connection* brilliantly shows you how."

—ALAINA LOVE
CEO, Purpose Linked Consulting
Author, *The Purpose Linked Organization: How Passionate Leaders Inspire Winning Teams and Great Results*
2021 Thought Leader of Distinction

THE
SEISMIC
SHIFT
IN
LEADERSHIP

HOW TO THRIVE IN A NEW ERA OF CONNECTION

THE SEISMIC SHIFT IN LEADERSHIP

MICHELLE K. JOHNSTON, PhD

WITH FOREWORD BY MARSHALL GOLDSMITH
NYT BESTSELLING AUTHOR, #1 LEADERSHIP THINKER

Advantage®

Published by Advantage, Charleston, South Carolina.
Member of Advantage Media Group.

ADVANTAGE is a registered trademark, and the Advantage colophon is a trademark of Advantage Media Group, Inc.

Printed in the United States of America.

10 9 8 7 6 5 4 3 2 1

ISBN: 978-1-64225-142-5
LCCN: 2021917901

Book design by Carly Blake.

This publication is designed to provide accurate and authoritative information in regard to the subject matter covered. It is sold with the understanding that the publisher is not engaged in rendering legal, accounting, or other professional services. If legal advice or other expert assistance is required, the services of a competent professional person should be sought.

Advantage Media Group is proud to be a part of the Tree Neutral® program. Tree Neutral offsets the number of trees consumed in the production and printing of this book by taking proactive steps such as planting trees in direct proportion to the number of trees used to print books. To learn more about Tree Neutral, please visit **www.treeneutral.com**.

TreeNeutral

Advantage Media Group is a publisher of business, self-improvement, and professional development books and online learning. We help entrepreneurs, business leaders, and professionals share their Stories, Passion, and Knowledge to help others Learn & Grow. Do you have a manuscript or book idea that you would like us to consider for publishing? Please visit **advantagefamily.com**.

To the city of New Orleans,
where you don't have to be perfect.

CONTENTS

ACKNOWLEDGMENTS. XIII

FOREWORD XV

INTRODUCTION. 1

PART 1. 7

CONNECTING WITH YOURSELF

CHAPTER 1. 9
Own Your Story, Your Narrative, Your Brand

CHAPTER 2. 29
Give Up Perfection

CHAPTER 3. 45
Own Your Communication Style

PART 2. 65

CONNECTING WITH YOUR TEAM

CHAPTER 4 67
Show Care and Compassion for the Whole Person

CHAPTER 5. 79
Listen to Lead

CHAPTER 6. 103
Act as a Servant Leader

PART 3 117

CONNECTING WITH YOUR ORGANIZATION

CHAPTER 7 119
Personally Align with Your Organization

CHAPTER 8 141
Create a Positive Culture

CHAPTER 9 161
Own Your Calendar

CHAPTER 10 171
Leaders Reckon with COVID-19

CONCLUSION 189

AFTERWORD 191

ACKNOWLEDGMENTS

Thank you to my daughter, Elizabeth, who gives me purpose, direction, and joy every single day of my life.

Thank you to my wonderful family: my father, who has *always* enthusiastically believed that I could do anything I wanted to do. And my brother, Chris, and his family—Pat, Steven, Sydney, Cole, and Addison—who provide unwavering love and support.

Thank you to my Loyola University New Orleans students who inspire me to be the best version of myself. To my Loyola colleagues who supported and rewarded me for being *me*. To Christina Jackson, my graduate assistant, whose tenacity, attention to detail, and beautiful spirit enabled me to finish this book. (You can read her transformational story in the Afterword.)

Thank you to Kittie Watson and Larry Barker of Spectra Consulting who saw something in me at the young age of twenty-two when they offered me an internship, which led to me falling in love with consulting and coaching.

Thank you to my incredible clients who showed me that being authentic, confident, and connected was the secret to successful leadership.

A huge thank you to Ochsner Health, where I got to witness extraordinary leadership during a global pandemic and multiple hurricanes. I'll never forget the poise and grace they modeled for their teams.

Thank you to my amazing girlfriends (coffee club, mom club, book club, walking club, wine club, high school besties, college roommates) who lift my spirits and offer the *best* advice on the many, many challenges of adulting.

I also owe gratitude to Brené Brown. If one of her and my dear friends, Eleanor Sharpe, had not given me the book *The Gifts of Imperfection*, I would not have been propelled to find my voice, own my story, and demonstrate authenticity. And without watching Brené deliver the University of Texas 2020 commencement speech on Zoom during a global pandemic, I would not have had the courage to publish this book.

FOREWORD

BY MARSHALL GOLDSMITH

A s an executive coach for over forty years, my mission has been to help successful people achieve positive, lasting change in behavior—for themselves, their people, and their teams. Over time, I have learned to look for a few critical components when it comes to improving trust and collaboration with leaders and their teams. These traits look different for each person, but all of these are vital to the success of the team and the organization as a whole. These traits are authenticity, communication, and connection.

As with all my material, what I teach is easy to understand yet difficult to do. You may assume that "authenticity" is a simple concept to understand, yet if you have been perceived as inauthentic, it can be very difficult to change this view in others. Where do you start?

One of the things that immediately drew me to *The Seismic Shift in Leadership* is that Michelle has created a guide to help you understand not only how to own your story, what your communication style is, and how you connect with your team, but also how to find and remove the barriers that may be preventing you from getting the maximum potential in your role.

As Michelle unpacks each of these segments to better connection, you'll notice that once broken down, what seems like a complex enigma becomes manageable and can be followed in a step-by-step process to a solution. You are guided not only by Michelle's personal experiences and research but also by the stories of so many incredible leaders and executives. These interviews reveal the real-life applications to these theories and how they can be applied in your office and team as well.

The Seismic Shift in Leadership is critical for leaders today as we move into a more digital and virtual working environment. With communication increasingly dominated by emails, texts, and virtual meetings, the importance of a leader's meaningful interaction with their team in these formats is greater than ever. Employees can feel disconnected from a leader who doesn't present themselves to their team in a way that makes them trustworthy and approachable. The organization can feel the lasting effects of miscommunication among teams due to a breakdown in communication styles. Leaders must be proactive to resolve these difficulties.

Michelle's research, methodologies, and expert examples create the perfect blend to apply these critical skills to your life. So read this book, apply it to your leadership, and watch the incredible results!

—Marshall Goldsmith
Thinkers50 Number One Executive Coach and *New York Times* best-selling author of *Triggers*, *Mojo*, and *What Got You Here Won't Get You There*.

INTRODUCTION

"Leaders are held hostage by how
other people perceive them."
—MARSHALL GOLDSMITH

n 2002, I read a *New Yorker* article[1] that changed the course of my life. The article was written by a journalist who followed Marshall Goldsmith, a leadership coach, around the country from executive to executive, chronicling his coaching style. Marshall typically worked with powerful chiefs who were successful at achieving results but not as successful at leading people. In fact, many of these leaders were seen as jerks, and some were at risk of losing their high-paying positions.

But somehow, after working with Marshall, these executives not only saved their jobs but also salvaged their relationships with their colleagues. How? They used Marshall's proven method of "feedforward."[2]

---

1   Larissa MacFarquhar, "The Better Boss," *New Yorker*, April 14, 2002, https://www.newyorker.com/magazine/2002/04/22/the-better-boss.

2   Marshall Goldsmith, "Try Feedforward Instead of Feedback," October 29, 2015, https://www.marshallgoldsmith.com/articles/try-feedforward-instead-feedback/.

1

Marshall met with each leader's key stakeholders and asked for suggestions on how the leader could improve moving forward. Then, after reviewing all the "feedforward" suggestions with Marshall, the leader met with each person who was interviewed, apologized for past mistakes, and asked for help in executing their action plan for improvement.

This article was my first introduction to Marshall, and I was blown away by his direct yet supportive approach for helping leaders improve. I could understand immediately why he was so successful, and I wanted to emulate his methodology. So I made a copy of the article and filed it away in hopes of using it as a blueprint for how I would one day serve as a leadership coach.

When the article was written, Marshall was listed as one of the five most respected executive coaches by *Forbes*. Little did I know that he would go on to be rated the number one executive coach in the world, rated number one global thought leader, a *New York Times* bestselling author, and a partner and supporter of my very first book on leadership—the one you are reading.

Years later, when I started consulting with high-level leaders, I dusted off the article and followed Marshall's proven methodology. Just like Marshall, I begin the coaching process by soliciting qualitative 360° feedback from the people who frequently interact with the leader from above, below, and across the organization (hence the name 360°). I ask questions about my client's leadership style, overall strengths, opportunities for improvement, and what success looks like. I then collapse all the qualitative data into a feedback report and share it with the leader to review. Typically, the leader finds the section on their opportunities for improvement to be very tough to read. But as tough as it is, seeing how your colleagues perceive you is a crucial and necessary step in a leader's development and one that provides an impetus to make the necessary changes for improvement. I tell all my leaders: with discomfort comes growth.

A few years ago, while coaching three different executives at three different companies, I had a eureka moment that prompted me to write this book. All three executives lost their jobs in the span of a few months. I was stunned and heartbroken, and I felt like I failed them. I asked myself, "How could I have coached them better?" I went back to their 360° feedback reports to look for patterns, themes, and answers. What surprised me was that all three of the reports had one common theme: each leader was perceived as *inauthentic, not trustworthy*. They were trying to be someone else, maybe their former boss or mentor. And they were leading with power and control, which created cultures of fear. This old "command and control" style of leadership built a fortified wall between them and their employees, resulting in a loss of trust. And we all know that once you lose trust with your team, you are no longer seen as a leader.

> **I TELL ALL MY LEADERS: WITH DISCOMFORT COMES GROWTH.**

Authenticity became imperative when the world went on lockdown during the COVID-19 crisis. Inauthentic leaders could no longer hide behind their office doors. Trust was needed more than ever before, because people were operating from a much more vulnerable place, often having to work from home. All of a sudden, the entire family was under one roof day after day. You were dressed in your casual clothes, sitting at the kitchen counter next to your children who were trying to learn online, amid dogs barking, babies crying, and spouses speaking over you.

Effective leaders immediately realized that they needed to emotionally connect with their teams during this stressful time. They needed to check in and ask, "How are you doing, really? How is your family doing? Are you taking care of yourself? How is your mental health?" These were questions that leaders didn't typically find themselves asking, but they became more and more necessary to make that meaningful connection with their teams who were displaced.

I'VE SEEN A SEISMIC SHIFT IN LEADERSHIP FROM *POWER* TO *CONNECTION*.

This is why I'm writing this book. I've seen a seismic shift in leadership from *power* to *connection*. I don't believe we will ever go back to the days of strict demarcation between people's professional and personal lives. Those lines became blurred as a result of the world going on lockdown, as organizational leaders entered homes to conduct business via video conferencing.

The old leadership characteristics of power, control, and fear are becoming more and more obsolete. Authenticity, compassion, and alignment are the new paths to leadership success. Is power necessary to demonstrate confidence? Yes, absolutely. Is power necessary to project a strong presence when making presentations? Yes, absolutely. But power needs to be redefined. A leader's new power lies in his or her ability to connect. The environment is more informal now, and flexibility will be the key moving forward. In order to keep their employees motivated in this new era, leaders will need to make an effort at genuine connection.

Connection can be divided into three foundational levels: connection with yourself, connection with your team, and connection with your organization. While leaders might consciously understand that connection is important, they don't necessarily know how or what to do. To many, connection is a nebulous concept. So to solve this problem, I interviewed eighteen leaders at large and small organizations across North America, South America, and Europe. I asked them to provide examples and stories of how they did or did not successfully:

- Connect with themselves

- Connect with their teams

- Connect with their organizations

After transcribing all the interview data, my graduate assistant, Christina Jackson, and I conducted a content analysis and identified the common themes in each of the foundational levels of connection.

The results show that the foundation of connection with yourself is *authenticity*, which includes the following steps:

- Own your story

- Give up perfection

- Own your communication style

The foundation of connection with your team is *compassion*, which includes the following steps:

- Show care and compassion for the whole person

- Listen first

- Act as a servant leader

The foundation of connecting with your organization is *alignment*, which includes the following steps:

- Personally align with your organization

- Create a positive culture

- Own your calendar

Why read this book? Why embrace connection? How will connection benefit you? Throughout my years as an executive coach and business professor, I have observed that leaders who connect successfully at all three of these levels have experienced the following benefits with their teams:

- Enhanced team cohesion

- Improved employee morale

- Higher job satisfaction

- Faster decision-making

- Increased productivity

This book is for any leader striving to be the best version of themselves. The goal in writing this book is to provide concrete examples for you, the leader, so you can get the best results in this new era of connection. After reading these stories, my hope is that you will feel empowered to project your authentic leadership style, to show compassion to your team, and to align yourself with your company.

Now, let's dive into the importance of connecting with yourself.

PART 1
CONNECTING WITH YOURSELF

"Be you, like no one else."
—LOYOLA UNIVERSITY NEW ORLEANS

IN THIS NEXT SECTION, you will hear from our fearless leaders about how they successfully connected (or didn't) with themselves. Specifically, you'll learn how to:

1. Own your story

2. Give up perfection

3. Own your communication style

CHAPTER 1

OWN YOUR STORY, YOUR NARRATIVE, YOUR BRAND

he *most important* level of connection is your connection with yourself. You have to figure out who you are to feel comfortable as a leader. Once you have that strong foundation and people see you as genuine, then you can more easily and effectively connect with others.

Connection with yourself involves owning your story, your narrative, your brand. Owning your story is about accepting the good, the bad, and the challenging times of your life. Rather than

> **THE *MOST IMPORTANT* LEVEL OF CONNECTION IS YOUR CONNECTION WITH YOURSELF.**

feeling self-conscious or ashamed of certain aspects of your life, the key is understanding that those difficult experiences made you who you are today. You've got to spend time figuring out how you grew and what you learned from going through those experiences. Because if you hide pieces of yourself, you are creating a barrier between you and those you interact with. Others might not be able to articulate what it is that's off, but they feel that something isn't right. Feeling shame and hiding parts of your life story create disconnection: disconnection with yourself and disconnection from others.

Dr. Brené Brown, a TED Talk phenom and University of Houston research professor, writes, "I now see how owning our story and loving ourselves through that process is the bravest thing that we will ever do. Courage, compassion, and connection only work when they are exercised. Every day." She goes on to say "We are wired for connection. It's in our biology. From the time we are born, we need connection to thrive emotionally, physically, spiritually, and intellectually. A decade ago, the idea that we're wired for connection might have been perceived as touchy-feely or New Age. Today, we know that the need for connection is more than a feeling or a hunch. It's hard science. Neuroscience to be exact."[3]

And right she was. Matthew Lieberman, a professor at UCLA, uses neuroscience to explain the human need for connection. In his book titled *Social: Why Our Brains Are Wired to Connect*, he found that social connection is so strong that when we are rejected or experience social pain, our brains "hurt" in the same way they do when we feel physical pain.[4] The bottom line is this: emotional pain resulting from a lack of connection is just as serious as physical pain. Human beings need connection to thrive.

I realized that if I were going to be as effective as I could be as an executive coach, I had to make sure I was connected with myself. And thinking back to my years of growing up, I realized I was *not* connected with myself. Since my family moved with General Motors

---

3   Brené Brown, *The Gifts of Imperfection: Let Go of Who You Think You're Supposed to Be and Embrace Who You Are* (Center City, Minnesota: Hazelden Publishing, 2010).

4   Matthew D. Lieberman, *Social: Why Our Brains Are Wired to Connect* (New York City: Crown Publishing Group, 2014).

every two years on average throughout my childhood, I remember some of my friends saying that they thought I was fake. I did not understand what they were talking about. But now I realize that when we moved from Alexandria, Virginia, to Baltimore, Maryland, to Memphis, Tennessee, to East Brunswick, New Jersey, to Rochester Hills, Michigan, to Tampa, Florida, to Birmingham, Alabama, my main focus was to fit in. I wanted to dress like my new friends, act like them, talk like them. I didn't know who I was, what my own identity was. Who was the real Michelle?

The most extreme example of trying to fit in is when I chose to attend Auburn University for college. I wanted to go to a traditional SEC university with a great football team and sororities and fraternities. I remember touring Auburn on a big football weekend when they were playing Georgia Tech. I'll never forget the parade going through little downtown Auburn and the cheer that the students were all yelling: "Wreck Tech! Wreck Tech! Wreck the heck out of Georgia Tech!" And then we went to the pep rally and football game, and I thought, *This is exactly what I had in mind for college!*

When I arrived at Auburn, I was recruited by one of the most Southern sororities, Kappa Delta. I loved all my pledge sisters and thought they were beautiful, kind, and graceful. I was in awe of their Southern style and mannerisms. So I donned the traditional Laura Ashley clothes and tried to hide my Northern accent and big Tampa hair (which there was no hiding!). Even though I tried very hard to fit in, I didn't feel like I did, and I'm sure others detected that as well. If I met someone from Virginia, I would say I was from Virginia. If I met someone who grew up in Alabama, I would say that my family lived in Birmingham. But I had only briefly lived in those places; I wasn't actually *from* any of those places. Looking back, I'm sure I gave off an inauthentic vibe. They couldn't get a good read on me because

11

I didn't have a keen sense of who I was. I was just trying to look and act like everyone else. I had become adept at fitting in but at the high cost of disconnection from myself and others.

This high cost became a powerful personal lesson when I received one of Brené Brown's books, *The Gifts of Imperfection*, as a birthday present. I'll never forget reading the first chapter of the book and bursting into tears. I don't mean that I teared up. I mean a waterfall of tears poured from my eyes! Brené's work had touched a nerve. Her research showed that the greatest barrier to belonging is fitting in. She said that when we try to fit in, we acclimate to the situation instead of standing for our authentic self. I wasn't able to be authentic because I didn't know who I was. I wasn't connected with myself. So I worked on owning my story, my narrative. Instead of feeling self-conscious that I moved around so much and didn't have a hometown, I changed my perception. I realized that, as a result of that particular upbringing, I was an open, adaptable, and resilient person. I changed the way I told my story to myself, and it positively affected how I interacted with others.

In my early years as an executive coach, I saw firsthand how important it was for leaders to have a strong connection with themselves. But sometimes when you grow as a person and as a leader, your story needs tweaking.

Meet Erika, a hard-charging, dependable, results-oriented leader. Her boss, the president of a media company, asked if I would coach her. He said he believed that Erika was talented enough to eventually move into the C-suite, but she didn't have the best reputation in the company. She was known to be impatient, demanding, and a little scrappy. She often rubbed people the wrong way and seemed unapproachable, with a chip on her shoulder. The president wanted his C-suite leaders to demonstrate executive presence, positivity, and a servant-leadership style. Erika needed some help.

When I sat down with Erika and asked about her story, she told me that she was a single mother who raised three daughters all on her own. As she described that part of her life, she seemed defensive and annoyed. "I did it all by myself, and so can others," Erika stated. The way she had been communicating with herself affected how she communicated with others. Now it all made sense to me where her demanding leadership style came from. Erika expected her staff to get the job done at whatever cost because *she* had always gotten the job done, whether on nights, weekends, or vacations or when she was sick. Those unrelenting expectations took their toll on her people.

When I asked Erika about her current situation, her face lit up as she shared that all three daughters had graduated from college and started their own careers and that she was recently engaged!

I explained that the story she was telling herself needed tweaking. Her script was outdated. I suggested that Erika rewrite the script to reflect her current situation: that she had raised and educated three daughters who were flourishing and that she had found a healthy relationship. The more compassion and kindness she could show to herself, the more compassion and kindness she would show to others. Her communication style would ultimately come across as more empathetic and understanding versus relentless and demanding. Ultimately, Erika ended up getting into the C-suite.

As Harvard Professor Frances X. Frei says, "You cannot change a person's behavior until you have first changed their belief." If the story you tell yourself is negative, it affects how you interact with the world at large. If you have scripts that are outdated running in your head on a continuous loop, they end up manifesting negative communication, whether in the words you use or in the body language you exhibit.

Leaders who are very hard on themselves tend to be even more demanding of those they lead. That is *not* the leader you want to be. So show yourself compassion. If you don't show yourself compassion, how can you expect others to? Own your story, your narrative. Think about your significant life experiences, what you learned, and how you grew. Think about how it made the brand called "you."

OWN YOUR STORY, YOUR NARRATIVE.

Now that you understand the importance of owning your story, in the next section you'll learn how leaders embraced their personal struggles to connect more authentically with themselves. Specifically, you'll hear from Kenneth Polite, John Nickens, Swin Cash, John Georges, and Julie Ibieta.

"Sharing the difficult, vulnerable pieces of your past will allow others to deeply connect with you on a very personal level. When you expose yourself as someone who has suffered in the same way that others have suffered, people will connect to you as a real person and as a real leader."

–KENNETH POLITE
ASSISTANT ATTORNEY GENERAL, CRIMINAL DIVISION, US DEPARTMENT OF JUSTICE

Now get ready for a powerful story of personal connection. Meet Kenneth Polite. Kenneth is someone who should be cocky and arrogant based on his extraordinary success in the legal world, but he remains a humble servant. I got to know Kenneth when he worked in New Orleans as the US Attorney for the Eastern

District of Louisiana from 2013 to 2017. As the chief federal law enforcement officer for Southeast Louisiana, he supervised the work of approximately fifty-five assistant US attorneys and was responsible for all criminal and civil matters, including political corruption, gang violence, narcotics distribution, healthcare fraud, human trafficking, civil rights violations, tax evasion, and environmental crimes.

Here's how Kenneth tells his own story:

So I was born and raised in New Orleans, born to teenage parents. My mom was sixteen years old when she had me and was living in housing projects in New Orleans. My father was seventeen at the time they got married. We grew up pretty poor in very poor areas of the city. I don't really remember living with my father. But I've got a pretty good relationship with him now as an adult. He was a police officer for thirty-seven years in New Orleans. And then you think about the fact that I became a US Attorney, and my brother is also a police officer. So my father, despite the fact that we didn't grow up with him in the household, definitely had an impact on his sons.

But the driving force for us was our mother. My mom ended up raising three boys by herself. We eventually spent most of our formative years growing up in the Lower Ninth Ward. It was a difficult neighborhood to grow up in. But my mom was always focused on our education, so we always went to Catholic schools. So I took a bus and a streetcar from my poor neighborhood to one of the fanciest, most expensive, and prestigious parts of our city to attend De La Salle High School. Traveling through such diverse neighborhoods was the start of my desire to bring communities together. And initially, my view was that I was having to straddle those communities. I felt I had to be a certain way when I was Uptown and then a different way when I was back hanging out with my friends in the Lower Ninth Ward. But then at some point, particularly as I was developing into leadership positions in high school, it became clear that my real purpose here was to try to connect those two lives.

During high school I started to embrace the notion of the service-oriented learning that the De La Salle tradition is built on. And we actually changed the name of the student council my senior year from "council" to "counsel." So "counsel" referred to advocating for other people, particularly for people who don't have that type of platform for themselves, like those from my old neighborhood. I ended up being both student body president and valedictorian, the first black student to be both of those in De La Salle's history. I went on to attend Harvard, which was very eye-opening, as you can imagine, coming from New Orleans.

In 2004, I lost my twenty-three-year-old half brother in a very violent death. We had the same father but different mothers. I did not grow up with my half brother in my life much of the time, but he was my brother.

I flew home from New York City, where I was practicing white-collar criminal defense at a private law firm. And I went to his house, and in his bedroom I saw that on one wall he had funeral programs of the twenty or thirty friends who had died before he had died. And then on the other wall he had special shirts that had been made for the funerals with the person's picture on it. I thought, *This is what he saw when he went to sleep at night and when he woke up in the morning, this imagery of death—in particular, of dying at a very young age.* And so this is what in many ways must have shaped his view of his own life and how he would ultimately pass away.

So I ended up putting together his funeral program, even though I didn't know him well. I was thinking here I was, a lawyer in New York, having gone through great halls of education and justice and courtrooms, yet somehow I wasn't able to shift the pathway of his life, somebody who was actually my own family.

That was when I decided I had to become a prosecutor to change this pattern in New Orleans. And we moved down to New Orleans in 2010.

Although Kenneth didn't tell his whole story to everyone he met early in his career, he learned from a mentor which pieces of his story to share.

One person I met was Lloyd Dennis, who founded a mentorship program called The Silverback Society, where African American professional men go into various schools to empower young men. When I met Lloyd, he said, "Tell me your story." After I told him about my brother, I remember him saying, "That's the piece of your story you have to remember to always talk about. Why? Because that is how people will connect to you as a real person, as a real leader with connections to this community, as someone who has suffered in the same way that others have suffered."

Kenneth realized that embracing his own narrative allowed him to connect with himself and with others in very authentic and effective ways.

"You must explore your story, capture all the
lessons there are to learn, and then own it."

—JOHN R. NICKENS IV

CEO, CHILDREN'S HOSPITAL NEW ORLEANS LCMC HEALTH

Now meet John R. Nickens IV, CEO of Children's Hospital New Orleans (LCMC Health). I was introduced to John by Tania Tetlow, a good friend, former neighbor, and now president of Loyola University New Orleans, where I serve on the faculty. Tania said that John was one of the best leaders she knew. So I set up an interview and was blown away by his story.

John joined LCMC Health as president and CEO in November 2017. During his time there, LCMC Health's pediatric market has experienced significant growth and achieved new highs in both patient experience and team member engagement scores. Prior to joining LCMC Health, John served as the executive vice president at Texas Children's Hospital in Houston.

John feels that successful leadership at the highest levels all goes back to owning your story. He believes you must be authentic and true to your values. You have to start there if you want to successfully connect with others and with your organization.

Here is John's story as he told it to me:

> We moved to Louisiana when I was a junior in high school in Tioga, across the river from Alexandria. During the very first couple of weeks, I'm trying out for football, and all the guys are talking about this girl who no one can date because her dad is the Southern Baptist preacher of the town. I'm a

newbie, so I'm a little overly bold, and I say, "I bet I can get a date with her."

And they're like, "Yeah, right." So bam! I get a date with her.

Two years later, she's pregnant. We're in our last couple of months of high school; she is eighteen and I am seventeen. Decision time. We have our life ahead of us. I was confident in a baseball scholarship for my next chapter, and she had a scholarship for singing to begin her college adventure. This was the late 1980s, and not many alternative programs existed for us, plus it was embarrassing to her Baptist Pastor father to have a daughter pregnant before marriage.

I went to my dad and said, "Marye's pregnant; we'll live with you guys."

And my dad responded with tough love. "No, you picked your road. Now go down it."

And I said, "Well, I didn't exactly pick it, I mean ..."

And he interrupted. "Yes. This is a consequence of choices you made. So now you get married. You go get a job."

And I'm like, "Well, what about my baseball scholarship?"

"This is a consequence of your decision. You don't get to do that; you don't get to *play* anymore. You get to work. It's time to grow up!"

This became a powerful life-changing moment that framed much of my thinking for decades to come. When you talk about stress in life, there are very few things that are more stressful than having to sit down with a Southern Baptist preacher and tell him that his daughter is pregnant. It was tough to feel like I failed my family and disappointed my dad, who was my hero.

When I think about connection with yourself, I believe you must own your story, explore it, and capture all the lessons to learn. Learning someone's story helps you better understand them, their background, and how and why they think a certain way. For me, this moment of failure and embarrassment created a confidence that I am not afraid to fail. In fact, I believe I already failed. I stutter-stepped into adulthood. I stumbled. I'm okay with that because I survived. I'm not afraid to say it. But the important part is to consider the failure and determine your response.

My dad said, "You picked your road; now go down it." Going down the road is what became my driver and daily catalyst to be better, to fail fast, and to learn fast. I took action. My first defining life lesson as an adult: **You can't always control what happens to you, but you can always control how you respond.**

John discussed the importance of identifying who you are early on:

As you get more and more successful, you should decide early in your career and personal life exactly who **you** are— your goals, your values. If not, other people will tell you who you are. **People will define your identity for you if you haven't already defined it.** People will have expectations that don't align with your core person. I think we all want to define the core principles of who we are—so do just that— spend time to think and decide.

Reflecting on your life lessons with an authentic desire to continue to listen, to learn, and to serve will guide you to the perfect career jobs. I have been purposeful through my career, and I am humbled for the privilege to serve at Children's Hospital. Knowing your skill set and strengths allows you to better connect with yourself and with the organization.

"I am a person who believes in authentic and genuine connection."

—SWIN CASH
VICE PRESIDENT OF BASKETBALL OPERATIONS AND TEAM DEVELOPMENT, NEW ORLEANS PELICANS

When I asked Greg Bensel, the senior vice president of communications for the New Orleans Saints and New Orleans Pelicans, which leaders in his organizations he thought best exemplified connection, he recommended that I speak with Swin Cash and Drew Brees.

Swin Cash is the vice president of basketball operations and team development for the New Orleans Pelicans. She is a retired professional basketball player who played for fifteen seasons in the Women's National Basketball Association (WNBA). In her second WNBA season, she led the Detroit Shock to their first-ever championship title, before she subsequently went on to win two more championships. Swin won a gold medal with the US women's basketball team at the 2004 Olympic Games and was inducted into the Women's Basketball Hall of Fame in 2020.

Swin Cash has an incredible personal story. She was raised in public housing outside of Pittsburgh by a mother who worked as a foreman doing manual labor.

I was raised to understand my faith for myself. I got to a point in high school where I had to figure out my core for myself. That's when I learned that my faith played a part in my life, and that was my foundation. But I also learned to accept other people for their different beliefs. Leading with love and care for other people is where my connection comes from. To lead with love is to lead with authenticity. So when you're talking about connections, I am a person who believes in authentic and genuine connection.

I asked Swin to talk about a significant life event that she feels made her into the successful basketball player and businesswoman she is today. She confided that a big turning point in her life came when she received some devastating news in 2007:

A few years ago, before I went back to the Olympics, I had a routine exam where the doctors were checking on a herniated disc in my back. Surprisingly, they found a small cancerous cyst that was on my kidney. So I had to go in and have surgery, which I found out right before the playoffs ...

I was a hot mess. We lost game five of the playoffs for the WNBA Championship. That was hard. And I remember this picture being taken of me, and there were all these stories asking, "Is this her last time in a [Detroit] Shock uniform?" It was a very tumultuous year for me. And people don't realize it, but that photo was very somber. At that moment, I wasn't thinking about basketball. I was thinking, *All right, now, you need to face what's coming next in life.* I remember looking back at that picture of me and thinking, *This is a moment that I look back on, and it's going to make me stronger.*

So eventually I requested a trade and left the team. I got the surgery done. But I remember that was a different point in my life, the first time I felt that there was something that I had no control over.

I had been completely healthy! We had just won the championship the year before. And only by the grace of God was the cancer found. So dealing with being completely healthy but then there's this thing that's in your body that can kill you. But the only way that you found it was by accident. That was a time when I had to hit the reset button and prepare for what was coming next.

I asked Swin how she became comfortable in her own skin.

I think that being truthful with yourself is probably the hardest thing to do. I'm not sure how I managed it. But sports have helped me be comfortable in my own skin. That's why I encourage so many people to get their kids involved in sports, because it taught me so much. I challenged myself to go through the wins and losses and things of that sort. It's kind of part of who I am. I also say that people need to seek out great mentors—I still do. I think at every level you should have a mentor or an advisor. I don't think you can ever get so big that you don't have one. Finally, make sure that you understand your environment, and make sure that people know you're real.

"Are you the person who is aspiring
to grow, or are you the person living
off of your earlier successes?"

–JOHN GEORGES

OWNER, *THE TIMES-PICAYUNE* AND *THE ADVOCATE*

In my early thirties, I gave a presentation on listening and communication at a Young Presidents' Organization meeting in WaterColor, Florida. I didn't know many of the young presidents in the audience, including John Georges, but he called me the very next week asking if I would help his company improve their overall communication. That consulting project was the beginning of a successful journey working with John as he grew his various businesses.

After majoring in business and accounting at Tulane University, John worked for Imperial Trading Company, which was started by his immigrant grandfather. He transformed his family's company to a billion-dollar corporation. I worked with several of John's leadership teams at his various companies and was a part of his executive transition team when he purchased Baton Rouge's newspaper, *The Advocate*, from the Manship family.

I sat down with John to learn more about how he connected with himself.

John said he always had a very strong connection with himself. "I have been the way I am since the age of eleven." He feels that he's never struggled with authenticity or with finding his leadership voice, owing in part to his upbringing:

> It's funny, someone wrote about me once, saying that I
> was always trying to prove myself. And I thought that was

kind of odd, because I've been authentically me since I was eleven years old.

My father drove a truck. It was for the family business, but he drove a truck home every night. I wanted to be a business-man; I wanted to be successful. But I didn't think of myself as a "leader."

I saw myself as a "worker." And I enjoyed the work. I would cut grass at the house one weekend and the other weekend go to work for my dad. I like to work, and I really connect with people who also like to work. Actually, I don't really enjoy what would seem to be the enjoyable parts of a job, the reaping of the benefits. I'd rather be working. An example is: today I ate a salad from Subway at my desk. I didn't go to Galatoire's.

Funny story, there used to be a spaghetti place called Tony's on Bourbon Street, and it was across the street from Gala-toire's. My father called Galatoire's "the fancy place." So my father and I would go into Tony's and get a plate lunch, in and out in less than thirty minutes. We'd look across the street at our competitor who was waiting in line at Gala-toire's. Obviously, they were far more successful than we were. And we were just the little guys. But the question is "Are you at Tony's or are you at Galatoire's?" Meaning, are you the guy who is aspiring to grow, or are you the guy living off your earlier successes? [John became the majority owner of Galatoire's in 2010.]

So I think I had a young ambition. My father and uncle were role models for me. To me, work was the thing, and I enjoyed it. And it really wasn't for the money, and it really wasn't for the things that money could buy. It was for the joy of actually working. They say if you open a restaurant to make money, you'll go broke. But if you open a restaurant because you love to cook, you'll make a fortune.

"Don't go to extremes to try and fit in to what the next culture is. You need to respect that culture and pick and choose what you like from it, but it is more important to come across as your genuine self instead."

–JULIE IBIETA
VARSITY VOLLEYBALL COACH, METAIRIE PARK COUNTRY DAY SCHOOL

While writing this book, I had the opportunity to work with the leaders and executive board members of Metairie Park Country Day School, a private K-12 school located outside of New Orleans. They told me that their varsity volleyball head coach, Julie Ibieta, had been named the Division V Coach of the Year for the tenth time, and that her team had not only won its eleventh state championship but had also been selected as the 2020 Allstate Sugar Bowl Greater New Orleans Girls Prep Team of the Year. So I immediately went to work to uncover the tricks of Julie's trade.

Julie discussed the importance of being an authentic and genuine leader:

When I first started coaching, I was an assistant coach in college. And I loved the head coach who I worked for. But when I went out on my own, I tried to be her a little bit. And my husband, who played sports his whole life, said, "You gotta find yourself." And so I made some mistakes, but as each mistake happened, I learned from them.

Julie talked about staying true to herself and to who she is:

You have to figure out who you are. That's the hard part. My husband and I have moved to three different parts of the country in the coaching realm. And we never changed as people. We lived in Lexington, Kentucky, we lived in Charlotte, North Carolina, and we currently live in New Orleans. All in the South, so I didn't go anywhere drastic, but they were all very different. And I never changed who I was. So I think that's important to come across as your genuine self. Not trying to fit in to what the next culture is. You need to respect that culture and pick and choose what you like out of that culture, but you need to not try and force yourself into it.

HERE'S WHAT WE'VE LEARNED

Now that you've heard from our leaders how important it is to own your story, I'd like for you to spend some time examining your past, your childhood, and your background. Most significant events that affect a person's character are struggles. Can you see how working through a difficult time helped you become the person you are today? Maybe that experience made you stronger, more resilient,

THAT'S THE KEY HERE: TO FIGURE OUT HOW A CHALLENGING LIFE EXPERIENCE GAVE YOU AN OPPORTUNITY TO GROW.

more compassionate, more empathetic. That's the key here: to figure out how a challenging life experience gave you an opportunity to grow.

What are some things in your past that you are self-conscious about? How can you show yourself compassion in how you handled those situations? Think about some of the events in your life: whether you were the protagonist or antagonist, whether they happened to you or whether you were the instigator. Now think about how you can demonstrate empathy for some of the choices you made in your life. Once you learn how to show yourself compassion, then you can show compassion to others.

REFLECTION AND ACTION

I want to help you connect with yourself by taking the time to answer the following questions:

1. What is a significant event that influenced who you are today?

2. What did you learn? How did you grow?

3. How did this event affect the way you lead?

4. Does that story sell you in a way that works for you?

5. Does your story need tweaking? If so, how?

CHAPTER 2

GIVE UP PERFECTION

Through working with countless leaders, I have found that the ones who think that they have to be perfect tend not to connect well with their teams. They think they have to dress perfectly, speak perfectly, write perfectly, and never make mistakes. They think that they have to appear infallible in order to rise up through the ranks of their organization. But based on my coaching experiences, I've learned that perfection equals disconnection.

Perfection = Disconnection

Research supports my observation. In Sally Helgesen and Marshall Goldsmith's recent book, *How Women Rise*, an entire chapter is dedicated to what they call "The Perfection Trap." They cite the following negative outcomes associated with a quest for perfection:[5]

1. Striving to be perfect creates stress for you and those around you.

---

5   Sally Helgesen and Marshall Goldsmith, *How Women Rise: Break the 12 Habits Holding You Back from Your Next Raise, Promotion, or Job* (New York City: Hachette, 2018).

2. Striving to be perfect keeps you riveted on details, distracting you from the big-picture orientation that's expected when you reach a senior leadership position.

3. Striving to be perfect creates a negative mindset in which you're bothered by every little thing that goes wrong, since even a small mistake can "ruin" the whole.

4. Striving to be perfect sets you up for disappointment for the simple reason that it's unrealistic. You, and the people who work with and for you, will never be perfect.

Leaders who try to be "perfect" tend to exert unrelenting pressure on their teams. This quest for perfection erects a wall between leaders and those they lead. This wall inadvertently creates a culture of fear.

In addition, I've observed that when these leaders see the faults of themselves in their people, they are extra hard. They don't give themselves or others permission to make

THE GOAL, AS WE WELL KNOW, IS CONNECTION, NOT PERFECTION.

mistakes. Establishing meaningful connection is difficult when your expectations are so high that few people can achieve them. The goal, as we well know, is *connection*, not perfection.

When I began my academic career as a twenty-eight-year-old visiting professor at Loyola University New Orleans, I wanted to be the perfect professor. But when I looked around the college of business, I didn't see one person who looked or acted like me. Most were older men who I found quite intimidating. But because I wanted to be the best, I asked a few of them if they would mentor me, and they kindly said yes.

My mentors and I met and mused on pedagogy and research. They gave me advice that had served them well. They told me to lecture for hours on end, give zeros for late work, and kick students out of the classroom if they were late. So I did. I became no-nonsense and serious, which was *not* my innate personality. I suppressed my natural characteristics of compassion, kindness, and enthusiasm and instead demonstrated a strict, masculine teaching style.

In order to appear credible as a young female professor, I thought I needed to project *power* in everything I did—how I dressed, how I spoke, how I taught. I preached the importance of never giving up your power. In fact, I remember when a student began her presentation by saying, "I'm sorry if I start coughing; I'm getting over a bad cold." After the presentation, when the class and I were giving her feedback, I said, "Don't ever say you're sorry. Don't mention that you are sick," almost as though being sick was a sign of weakness.

Around the same time, I was teaching a class to undergraduate students about nonverbal communication. In the middle of my lecture, one of my heels flew off my foot high into the air, somersaulted, and landed ten feet away. Without saying a word, I calmly hopped over on one foot, slid the heel back on, and continued lecturing without mentioning what had just happened. I thought that acknowledging a mishap made you appear weak. To succeed, I thought I had to be all-powerful, at all times, at whatever cost.

So I shouldn't have been surprised when I received poor faculty evaluations. But I was. I was surprised, shocked, and upset. So I did what every book tells you *not* to do as a female professional: I marched straight into the associate dean's office and cried! I had tears running down my cheeks as I asked, "What am I doing wrong?"

In order to receive tenure and promotion, I knew I had to improve my teaching evaluations. But what my colleagues and I didn't realize was that pretending to be perfect would never work. I had to give up trying to seem infallible. I had to feel comfortable in my own skin as a young, energetic former gymnast and cheerleader. Yep, cheerleader.

I now admit it, but for years as a young professor, I didn't disclose that I flipped my way across basketball courts and football fields in junior high and high school. I thought I would lose credibility.

In addition to receiving above-average teaching evaluations, one of the other tenets of academic life is "publish or perish." While I was working on a research paper with one of my colleagues, Dr. Kendra Reed, I came across a study that found that the most important characteristic that differentiated high-performing teams from low-performing teams was having at least one female on the team.[6] Finally, *finally*, a light (a huge flash, actually) went on in my head. "Wait," I thought. "Perhaps I really could be myself in the business classroom. Perhaps being a woman and demonstrating more feminine traits could actually be an asset and not a liability!"

So it was that day that I made significant changes. I tossed out my look of black Ann Taylor pantsuits, reasonable shoes, hair tied in a low ponytail with little makeup and limited jewelry, trying to emulate my male colleagues. I started to wear dresses and skirts and heels and makeup from my earlier days working for Spectra, a consulting firm. I displayed my natural qualities of empathy, warmth, and kindness to the students. I told them I was there to find their strengths, not their weaknesses. I was there to support them, to help them succeed. And I was not going to apologize for being too nice, too energetic, or too happy anymore. I was going to be 100 percent me, Michelle Kirtley Johnston.

And wouldn't you know it? My teaching evaluations significantly improved. In fact, a few years later I won the MBA top teaching award. I had been on a quest for perfection my whole life. But now I

---

6   Otti Jõgi, "9 Unique Traits of High Performing Teams," Weekdone.com, accessed July 14, 2021, https://blog.weekdone. com/9-unique-traits-of-high-performance-teams-infographic/.

finally realized that trying to be anything but me was a disadvantage to being a good leader. I didn't have to be perfect. What I had to be was *me*.

A few years later I encountered a client who struggled with perfection like I once did. I was asked to coach Anne, an interim CEO of an oil and gas company. Anne had been mentored by her tough-as-nails CEO for fifteen years. This former CEO was direct and demanding, but his team trusted him and thought he was effective. So Anne emulated his leadership style. But when she and I reviewed her 360° feedback report, there was a look of shock on her face. The feedback was negative and harsh. Her team found her to be overly aggressive. Her style came across as controlling, defensive, and critical of others. She ruled with power and fear. As a result, her team was scared of her.

> ## I DIDN'T HAVE TO BE PERFECT. WHAT I HAD TO BE WAS *ME*.

Adam Galinsky's research out of Columbia University uncovered that when you are in a position of power, your "whisper is a shout."[7] Everything you say and do is amplified, often in a negative way. Anne didn't even realize that many of her actions were interpreted harshly by her team. For example, when she walked across the department floor and said, "Mark, could you stop by my office at two o'clock?" Mark immediately feared that he was getting fired. Or when Susan texted Anne asking for a project update but never heard back, Susan assumed that Anne was unhappy with her work.

After spending some time with Anne, it was clear to me that Anne thought she had to be all-powerful. And it was her downfall. What she didn't realize was that power wasn't the answer; *connection*

---

7   Adam Galinsky, "When You're in Charge, Your Whisper May Feel Like a Shout," *The New York Times*, August 15, 2015, https://www.nytimes.com/2015/08/16/jobs/when-youre-in-charge-your-whisper-may-feel-like-a-shout.html.

was the answer. But Anne had lost the necessary connection with her team to be successful. She decided to resign a few months later.

Tim, a marketing executive based out of Atlanta, was similarly *relentless* in his quest for perfection. Tim demanded perfection from himself and from his team. His suits were impeccably tailored. He never had a hair out of place. He had a magnetic, pearly white smile. He looked the part of a successful executive. But when you scraped below the surface in his division, you discovered that turnover was high and satisfaction was low. Tim was brilliant at achieving, even surpassing, company goals, but he wasn't well respected as a leader.

Tim asked me to help him facilitate a leadership development meeting for his team. Our topic was how to create an environment that sparked innovation. We were asking his leaders to demonstrate compassion and empathy in order to create an environment where employees felt safe enough to take risks.

I quickly realized that Tim was not going to have credibility with his team if he couldn't demonstrate the characteristics of compassion and empathy that he was asking of his leaders. I recommended that he begin by sharing a challenging time in his life when he made a mistake. In the past, Tim never would have shared *any* personal information, let alone a time when he struggled. He would have viewed that as weak. In his mind, he was supposed to be a model of perfection. And perfect leaders don't make mistakes, let alone admit them. But thankfully, Tim complied and kicked off the leadership meeting with a personal story of when he struggled and made a big mistake. Afterward, his team thanked him for opening up and showing them that he was human and fallible. They felt a sense of relief that perhaps they didn't have to be so perfect. That perhaps they, too, could take risks and occasionally make mistakes in an effort to innovate.

As we emphasized earlier, perfection creates disconnection.

When leaders think they have to appear infallible, a barrier is created between them and their team. Instead of encouraging employees to excel, perfection breaks down trust. Employees feel demoralized and sometimes abused. These cultures of fear can even create unhealthy competition between team members. No one wants to be the bad apple in the leader's eyes. Rather than acting as a cohesive team, each member competes against one another to be viewed as the winner, the favorite, the top performer.

My advice: give up the quest for perfection. Own your fallibility, warts and all.

Now, I hope you understand the negative consequences of an obsession with perfection. Next, you'll read stories from our leaders explaining how abandoning their desire to be perfect was a necessary step in truly connecting with themselves. Specifically, you'll hear from Tania Tetlow, Juan Martin, and Robért LeBlanc.

> "Focus on acting bravely instead of striving for perfection. Perfectionism makes it more difficult to connect due to a lack of vulnerability."
>
> **—TANIA TETLOW**
> PRESIDENT, LOYOLA UNIVERSITY NEW ORLEANS

Tania Tetlow and I were friends and moms raising our daughters in the same neighborhood before she was persuaded by multiple people to put her name in the hat to become the president of Loyola University New Orleans. I have a vivid memory of Tania and me preparing for her upcoming interviews with the search committee.

We were talking about the odds that the committee would choose not only the very first layperson but the very first female to serve as president of Loyola. I told Tania, "Don't get your hopes up; it probably won't happen." *Thank goodness* I was wrong! I'm embarrassed now that I even shared that sentiment out loud. Looking back, I hope my skepticism gave Tania even more motivation to win the job because Tania is an exceptional leader with rare gifts of connection.

Prior to becoming the president of Loyola in 2018, Tania was a federal prosecutor, a commercial litigator, and a law professor. She graduated cum laude with a bachelor of arts from Tulane University and magna cum laude from Harvard Law School.

Tania and I sat down and talked about her role as the first female leader of a one-hundred-plus-year-old Jesuit institution.

"As girls, we are trained to be perfect rather than brave," she states. She learned early on that if she just focused on "pretty good" instead of being "perfect," her pretty good was still damn good. "I used to make myself sing solos in public because then I wouldn't be so afraid of doing public speaking. I was singing a solo in church once, and I totally screwed it up. And I had an epiphany 'Oh, they like me more, not less, now. They're with me; they're not mad at me.'" When the audience noticed that Tania had erred in her solo, the audience was more invested in her than if she had sung the piece perfectly.

Perfectionism makes it harder for women to connect because there's a lack of vulnerability. Women are trained to be likeable, but self-deprecation gives away power. She says that she has seen many female leaders who "self-flagellate." Instead, they must figure out how to be confident without being arrogant.

I had a beloved colleague whose *only* hurdle was that she self-deprecated so often. She was being considered for a promotion, and I kept hearing, "She's a rock star, but why does she keep putting herself down?" It was the only thing standing in her way.

It's okay to self-deprecate. It can be very endearing, and it's part of showing vulnerability, but I choose subjects that don't matter. I will tease myself for being the worst bowler in human history (and for once getting a strike in a lane that was not my own!) because nobody cares how I bowl.

In other words, while Tania is a bad bowler, she would never put herself down or make fun of an inadequacy that is paramount to her job. "I think that connection is a function of self-knowledge. If you are driven by pride, you will put people off because they can tell. They can sniff that out."

Tania learned a lot about leadership from Lindy Boggs, the first woman elected to Congress from Louisiana. "Lindy's fuel (which was limitless) was that she just found other people so interesting." Discovering similarities is easier if you genuinely enjoy people. If you recognize that everyone has a story, and you're interested in his or her story, then you will have an immediate commonality.

"The more perfect you think you are, the more imperfect you are. The more you can come to terms with the imperfections you have, the better, more rounded you become."

–JUAN MARTIN

GLOBAL PRESIDENT, KIND SNACKS AND NATURE'S BAKERY

I met Juan Martin, the global president of KIND Snacks, while attending a virtual annual meeting of global CEOs, thought leaders, and executive coaches. Juan was one of the featured speakers, and when he spoke about his leadership role, you could feel his compassion and kindness through the computer screen. Before serving in his present position, Juan ran Mars, Inc.'s multibillion-dollar portfolio of pet care, food, chocolate, and chewing gum in fifty-two countries in Europe and Africa. Juan is a values-driven, passionate, and authentic global executive who is a true people leader.

I reached out and interviewed Juan, curious to discover his secrets of leadership connection. When asked which level of connection he struggled with, Juan's answer surprised me.

The level of connection that took me the longest to get right was connection to myself. I think self-awareness was the biggest enabler for me. But in order to truly connect to the real me, I had to confront my own demons. And it took me a while. During the last seven years of my life, since my mom passed away, it's been a completely different story of how I connect to myself, how aware I am of my strengths and my weaknesses, and at the end of the day, what makes me human. This self-awareness journey was not an easy ride for me.

For years, I had chosen to live with the facade of who Juan was. We have been educated as kids to show certain types of behaviors and to hide others. I was raised in a Spanish culture where, as men, we were supposed to demonstrate confidence; we were not supposed to disclose vulnerabilities, we were not to cry in public, we were to be very aggressive in order for our opinions to be taken into consideration. So there were a lot of assumptions and prejudgments on how you should or should not behave. And obviously, you practice that muscle for fifteen, twenty years, and you end up being good at what you do, which is a combination of who you are but also what you fake to the world. When I look back on my career, I realize I had a knot inside of me. There was something not working for me. I always found good excuses for why I shouldn't hire a leadership coach and escaped from having mentors. And those were my defense mechanisms.

So when I looked at your own levels of connection, Michelle, I was not connecting with myself at all. I don't know if I'd call it fake or artificial, but for sure it didn't feel truly ingrained and authentic. And I think there are a lot of leaders who fake it. And they fake it really well, but there is a limiting factor there. Those people don't allow themselves to show what they're able to do to their maximum potential. Because they become so trained in one way of working and, basically, they cannot go beyond that. I'm sure they have much more to offer. But they've been suppressed by certain habits, or certain expectations, or certain fake stipulations that somebody told him or her they needed to portray.

Those people are smart people. But funny enough, they measure themselves out of no substance. Because the more perfect you think you are, the more imperfect you are. The more you can come to terms with the imperfections you have, the better, more rounded you become. It's as simple as that. I have a saying that I use with organizations, which goes like this: "A-leaders recruit A-people. B-leaders recruit C-people." Because the last thing that B-leaders want to have is a B-player to potentially compete with them, much less an A-player. That's okay if one person does it. But when you think about the systemic implications of B-leaders hiring C-players throughout an organization, it's the beginning of the end.

"I don't believe in perfectionism; I believe in excellence."

–ROBÉRT LEBLANC
FOUNDER, CEO, AND CREATIVE DIRECTOR, LEBLANC+SMITH

Let me introduce you to Robért LeBlanc, founder and creative director of LeBLANC+SMITH Hospitality Group, a boutique collection of restaurants and bars. The team entered the hotel scene in 2020 with The Chloe, a fourteen-room food- and beverage-driven hotel in Uptown New Orleans. Robért was named 2019 Restaurateur of the Year by the Louisiana Restaurant Association.

Robért revealed that his underdog mentality got in the way of finding his authentic leadership voice.

What was most important to finding my authentic leadership voice was overcoming a characteristic of my behavior and personality that's really not healthy, from a professional or personal standpoint: my underdog mentality.

I held on to this idea that my back was against the wall, and I had to fight out of a corner. But in those underdog situations, I always felt I performed at my best, my clearest. In hindsight, though, that underdog mentality got in the way of my authentic leadership. It was not until I overcame that mentality that I became fully comfortable in my own skin and capable of leading.

I also learned to be unapologetic about doing what I felt strongly needed to be done. My greatest moments of growth and prosperity, not in a financial sense but in the sense of productivity, were in reaction to Hurricane Katrina and in reaction to the COVID-19 pandemic. When the odds are against me, that's when I do my best work, primarily because that is when I need to be most decisive and trust my own instincts. That's when I get in the mind space and learn to be unapologetic about my choices or decisions because it is literally a matter of survival.

During Katrina, we lost everything. Putting it back together created this trajectory, then when things started going smoothly, I felt like I didn't deserve it. And that mindset that we all have when we're kids, particularly growing up in the South, is that "it's got to be hard to be valuable." So when it stopped being hard, and it was still productive, it didn't feel right. And I felt guilty, and I probably self-sabotaged to make it harder. But I've conditioned myself to be really good and to be unflinching and unyielding when I'm facing impossible odds. And so that's what it was: the environment forced me to own it and to be unapologetic. I need to figure out how I can continue to be that prolific when I'm not against impossible odds.

Eventually, Robért learned to strive for excellence over perfectionism.

Finding my voice wasn't conscious design; it was sort of that idea of "unconscious incompetence." I didn't know what I didn't know. But if you asked me right now, at forty-three, to reflect on that, I think that my relationship with you as my former professor is indicative of my journey. I was fortunate enough to have teachers, coaches, and mentors like you who I really trusted and respected, who believed in me before I believed in myself. I truly feel that self-belief starts with others' belief in you. You all saw something in me that I had not yet seen in myself. I trusted and believed in you, and through your lens I began to believe in myself.

The second thing that helped me to develop an authentic leadership voice was learning from my own mistakes. I wouldn't say that I was a perfectionist, but I used to be so afraid to make mistakes when I was younger. Over time, I have learned the value of being decisive and not being afraid of making mistakes. That just making a decision is more valuable than the avoidance of mistakes. If you make a tough choice that turns out correctly, it builds your experience base and it builds confidence. But if you make that tough choice and it's the wrong one, that mistake provides an invaluable learning and development lesson too.

I don't believe in perfectionism; I believe in excellence. And I think the distinct difference is that while you never really want to make mistakes, mistakes are a crucial part of life. If you believe in excellence, you allow for some mistakes. Perfectionism allows for no mistakes. As such, perfectionism creates a tremendous amount of stress and anxiety. It creates a fear that leads to indecision. There is literally no such thing as a "perfect thing," even in science and art there's no such thing as a perfect thing. People who pride themselves on being perfectionists typically don't go very far because they can't dig in and make the tough decisions that it takes to succeed.

The goal is progress. Whatever it is, if you're building something, creating something, leading something, the goal is to get to the best outcome. And you want to do that as quickly as possible. But what happens when you are a perfectionist is that you sit on the sidelines for three or four weeks

THE GOAL IS PROGRESS.

constantly worried about whether or not your decision is perfect. However, if you made a quick decision in four days instead and soon realized that it was the wrong decision, you're there in a week as opposed to four weeks. That makes all the difference in the world when you start compounding the time line. That's why decisiveness is so crucial. And decisiveness comes from a connection with yourself.

HERE'S WHAT WE'VE LEARNED

L eaders who believe that they have to appear perfect at all times are not perceived as authentic. They are seen as disingenuous, fake, and insincere. The quest for perfection creates a barrier between leaders and those they lead. Leaders who try to be perfect also tend to exert unrelenting pressure on their teams, thereby creating cultures of fear, which lead to disconnection and competition between team members. The more quickly you can come to terms with the imperfections you have, the better and more rounded you'll become.

REFLECTION AND ACTION

Now, think about how perfection equals disconnection.

1. Have you struggled with trying to seem perfect as a leader? If so, how did it affect your team?

2. What are some things that you can do to show that you aren't perfect and that you don't demand perfection?

3. Do you allow for mistakes?

4. Have there been times when you might have inadvertently created a culture of fear with your team?

5. How can you create a culture of connection?

CHAPTER 3

OWN YOUR COMMUNICATION STYLE

The next step to effectively connect with yourself is to understand your individual communication style.

Why does it matter whether or not you embrace your specific communication style? Because we all communicate differently. And to motivate their teams, leaders must figure out how to best connect with each team member. If you can't connect with someone at their level in a way that makes sense to them, then it doesn't matter how effectively you *think* you communicate. As the late Stephen Covey, a *New York Times* bestselling author said, "The only message that counts is the one that's received."[8]

Many different communication styles exist. Some people prefer to connect at a relational level. They ask lots of questions about your background and your family because they're interested in you on a personal level. In turn, these types of people will often share a lot about themselves in hopes of forming a bond. Other communicators might not be that interested in the personal details. They are very

---

8   Steven R. Covey, *Seven Habits of Highly Effective People* (New York City: Free Press, 1989).

task-oriented and want to know what they need to do by when. They speak and listen in bullet points. Or some communicators love to talk about research and data. They are great proofreaders and don't want to make decisions before they have all the facts. Finally, some communicators would rather send a text or an email versus speaking face-to-face.

I witnessed the consequences of communication breakdowns throughout my time working with Spectra, the consulting firm that recruited me while I was getting my master's degree at Auburn University. While consulting with large companies including Pfizer and Entergy, the number one complaint I heard time and time again was communication, or the lack thereof.

Larry Barker and Kittie Watson, the respective president and vice president of Spectra, had developed an inventory called the Listener Preference Profile (LPP) that identified four different listening styles. The LPP became the backbone of many of my research articles and training seminars. However, I wanted to focus on overall communication style, not just listening style. I got my chance when I went on my first sabbatical as a tenured university professor in 2011 and developed the Communication Preference Profile (CPP) with Kittie and Larry.

Hundreds of different communication inventories are on the market, but I'm going to discuss the four styles identified by the CPP, only because I know it so well. If you would like to complete the inventory that most aligns with the content of this book, you can visit https://innolectinc.com/product/communications-preference-profile/.

The four communication styles (or preferences) form the acronym PACT, which stands for people, action, content, and technology. After you take the CPP, the results will explain your dominant communication preference.

If your dominant communication preference is people-oriented, then your communication is driven by relationships. When connecting, you tend to:

- Focus on the relationship during conversations.

- Provide clear verbal and nonverbal feedback.

- Find areas of common interest.

If your dominant communication preference is action-oriented, then your communication is driven by results. When connecting, you tend to:

- Focus on the bottom line.

- Jump ahead and finish thoughts of speakers.

- Get frustrated by unorganized and rambling speakers.

If your dominant communication preference is content-oriented, then your communication is driven by information. When connecting, you tend to:

- Welcome complex and challenging information.

- Look at all sides of an issue.

- Use facts and evidence in making persuasive arguments.

If your dominant communication preference is technology-oriented, then your communication is driven by efficiency. When connecting, you tend to:

- Favor efficiency and speed when sending and receiving messages.

- Enjoy keeping up with new communication technologies.

- Prefer to communicate through email or text rather than face-to-face.

Whether your dominant communication style is people-, action-, content-, or technology-oriented, or a combination, let me share some real-world examples of how style differences can potentially hinder communication effectiveness.

Meet Tommy, the chief of development at Tri-State, Inc. I was enlisted to coach Tommy on his executive presentations. After I observed a number of them, the first thing I said to Tommy was, "Who was that person on stage? Because it wasn't you." After talking with Tommy, I realized that he was trying to emulate someone else's presentation style: the CEO of Tri-State.

The CEO was a high content-oriented communicator who valued data and evidence. He used data analytics and quantitative research for each point that he spoke about. Each slide in his presentation had three or four charts or graphs showing data trends. So when Tommy started making executive presentations for the company, he simply used the CEO's templates to mimic the CEO's style.

To begin our work together, I took Tommy through the first step of the connection model. The goal was to get him comfortable with who he was and what he brought to the table. As we have learned, people trust their leader if they find him or her authentic. And the path to authenticity is owning your story.

I then took Tommy through the second step, which was to own his communication style. After he completed the Communication Preference Profile, we learned that Tommy was a high people-oriented, high action-oriented communicator. He scored low in the content-oriented communication style. These findings explained why delivering a high-content presentation, like the ones his CEO delivered, wasn't the correct fit for his personality and skill set.

Now that Tommy understood that he was a people and action communicator, we reworked his two upcoming presentations: a town hall speech and a large executive strategy speech.

In order to capitalize on his specific communication strengths, we sought ways to connect with the audience and get them motivated to execute. So for the town hall presentation to his entire division, Tommy grabbed the audience's attention by beginning with a personal story about himself. He injected humor and self-deprecation to show he was human and relatable. He then used pictures and short videos instead of utilizing graph after graph. He shared vivid examples of employee stories to support his points. At the end of his presentation, he had a "call to action" to galvanize his employees and get them excited about reaching the organization's goals.

Next, Tommy was asked to deliver a presentation to five thousand employees at Tri-State's annual leadership meeting. I sat in the back of the grand ballroom to watch. When he got up to speak at this large gathering, Tommy smiled, got out from behind the podium, and engaged the audience. He wanted to encourage the employees to take risks (sometimes failing in the process) in order to innovate. So he told a story of how he "failed fast" the previous year when he took a huge risk to try to innovate and diversify the company's portfolio. He was clearly comfortable in his own skin. You could tell he was relaxed and enjoyed connecting with the audience. This new and improved presentation style was a 180-degree change from the first time I saw him speak at a big meeting.

Next, we worked on how Tommy ran his employee meetings. When he was new to Tri-State, the CEO told him to develop a strong "meeting rhythm." Tommy learned that his meeting rhythm needed to include the following:

- One-on-one meetings with direct reports once every two weeks

- Team meetings at least once a month

- Morning huddles at least once a week

- Town hall meetings every quarter

Tommy had previously worked at a small family-owned company where they rarely held meetings at all, so this was a new concept for him. In his first few months at Tri-State, Tommy spent most of his time in meetings discussing strategy, goals, and initiatives like other executives did. Tommy was an introvert by nature and known to be a very good listener. So two hours of nonstop talking made him feel like he was just a talking head. He didn't feel like he was connecting with the people on his team. He wanted to switch things around. So we sat down to talk about his meeting goals and how they could better align with his communication style:

- Goal 1: Tommy wanted to understand how each individual on his team was doing so that he could remove barriers and help them succeed.

- Goal 2: Tommy wanted to build a unified and cohesive team.

- Goal 3: Tommy wanted to give his direct reports clear marching orders.

Tommy's first priority was to meaningfully connect with each individual on his team, because he felt that he wouldn't get the desired results if he didn't understand their headspace. Tommy wanted to know what made his leaders tick, how exhausted or stressed they were, and what they thought was working and not working.

So in order to play to Tommy's strengths as a communicator, we flip-flopped the agenda of the meetings. Now, at the beginning of every team meeting, he spends twenty minutes going around the room and asking, on a scale of one to ten, how each leader is feeling in their personal and professional lives. This exercise checks the box of Tommy's desire to get the pulse of his team.

Second, in order to promote team collaboration, Tommy selects one leader each month to share their current projects with the team. He asks how these projects are coming along, their ultimate goals, and if they need help from anyone at that table, including himself.

Lastly, Tommy closes out the meetings with important company updates and necessary action steps to achieve the current goals.

As you can see, Tommy moved from the conventional model of 80 percent talking to 80 percent listening. He now spends most of the meeting time asking questions, learning what his team members need from him, and helping them with their challenges.

Tommy's meetings soon became the talk of the company. Leader after leader often asks to be under Tommy's tutelage because of the way he cares, listens, and supports his employees.

Tommy's communication strategy is supported by research from Daniel Shapiro, a Harvard Business School professor who teaches negotiation. Shapiro found that if you spend time finding commonality and connection within and among your team, relationships form and strengthen.[9] And other studies have found that teams with strong relationships make decisions twice as fast with half the number of meetings.[10]

Next, I'd like to share an example of how opposing communication styles can negatively affect work relationships and hamper decision-making. When I was consulting with a nonprofit organization, two leaders, Jake and Sam, had to work closely together but struggled with their interactions. In fact, their interactions became

---

9   Daniel Shapiro, *Negotiating the Nonnegotiable: How to Resolve Your Most Emotionally Charged Conflicts* (New York City: Penguin Books, 2017).

10   Erik Larson, "New Research: Diversity + Inclusion = Better Decision Making at Work," *Forbes*, September 21, 2017, https://www.forbes.com/sites/eriklarson/2017/09/21/new-research-diversity-inclusion-better-decision-making-at-work/.

so tense that each leader circumnavigated the organization to work around each other rather than with each other.

Jake worked in communications and was a content-oriented communicator. He was highly detailed and obsessed with grammar. Jake planned, researched, and provided lots of data in his messages. "I spend a lot of time putting together my emails, sharing context, background, data, and evidence, and I find it rude when someone responds with one sentence with misspelled words."

On the other hand, Sam, who worked in strategy and business development, was an action-oriented communicator. He was a bottom line, results-oriented leader who viewed situations from thirty-three thousand feet. Sam often sent brief, blunt messages when emailing. He explained his style by saying, "I don't worry about spelling or grammar because my emphasis is on getting the job done. I don't want to spend a lot of time worrying about the details."

Sometimes Sam didn't even respond to Jake's lengthy emails. And when Sam ignored those emails, Jake felt disrespected. The end result, as you can imagine, was frustration and inefficiency. Why inefficiency? Because Jake ended up going around Sam to get his work done due to Sam's lack of communication.

Which leads to how I got involved. I happened to serve as both Sam and Jake's leadership coach. So I was very aware of their differences and frustrations with each other. That's why I decided to facilitate a meeting between the two of them. I asked them to explain how they interpreted each other's communication styles. Jake went first.

Jake reiterated that he spends a lot of time sharing context, data, and evidence when composing his emails. He said, "I find it rude when Sam just ignores the emails."

Sam responded, "I'm not trying to be disrespectful at all; I'm just trying to get things done in the most efficient way possible. I rarely have time to go through so many paragraphs trying to find what exactly you want me to do."

Jake needed Sam's approval on certain projects in order to do his job, so he asked Sam, "What can I do to get you to read and respond to my emails?"

Sam said, "If you want me to read your emails and act on them, tell me what you need from me in the very beginning of the email. Then give me the necessary information in three bullet points. Include the data and support in the last paragraph so that I can review it if I need to."

Jake responded, "You got it!"

By the end of the meeting, Sam and Jake were both laughing about their negative interpretations of each other. Now, they recognized that their opposite communication styles were what got them into trouble.

I recommended to Sam and Jake that they follow my mantra: "To respond is to respect." When you respond to an email or text, you are **"TO RESPOND IS TO RESPECT."** demonstrating respect to that person. Often, leaders don't recognize how powerful their actions *and* inactions are. Because as we said earlier, humans assume the worst. Leaders are usually surprised to hear this. So I ask all leaders that I coach to at least acknowledge that they received communication. They can say "got it" or "okay" or "thank you"; they don't have to provide an answer immediately—just acknowledge that they received the text or email. Acknowledgment reduces false assumptions and misinterpretations.

After the meeting, Sam and Jake were able to bridge their communication differences and now communicate much more effectively. Each leader is more satisfied and more productive.

Now, let's learn from our leaders how they owned their individual communication styles to effectively connect with themselves and others. Specifically, you'll hear from Pete November, Jim L. Mora, and Warner Thomas.

"Acknowledging that you're not the best in some aspect creates connection. Instead of demonstrating that you're in competition with your peers, show them that you're caring, compassionate, and open. Then it becomes like two really good friends trying to figure a problem out."

–PETE NOVEMBER

EXECUTIVE VICE PRESIDENT AND CHIEF FINANCIAL
OFFICER, OCHSNER HEALTH

I have had the privilege of serving as Pete November's executive coach for many years now. Pete is one of the most gifted leaders I have ever worked with. I can't tell you how many people say to me, "Michelle, can you figure out a way that I can work under Pete? I want to learn how to be an exceptional leader from him."

Pete was recently promoted at the end of 2020 to chief financial officer of Ochsner Health, the largest nonprofit healthcare system in Louisiana. Formerly he served as the chief administrative officer where he managed shared services including innovation, digital medicine, telehealth, supply chain, system partnerships and integration, and real estate.

Pete has a true understanding that genuine connection is the essence of great leadership. He stresses to his team every opportunity he gets that collaboration, listening, and empathy are the necessary ingredients to leadership success.

> I think that if a person in their soul is a caring person, and values relationships with other people, and has a desire to help and watch others succeed, they will be a great leader. But I think if you have someone who is not caring at their core and is more focused on themselves and what they achieved, and isn't really concerned about other people's feelings and relationships, I don't think you can make them a great leader. I think they can get things done, but they're not going to be a great leader.

> One of the necessary components in owning your communication style is that you must become aware of your blind spots. For example, I'm a big picture, action-oriented leader. I surround myself with people who are more cautious than me and focused on the process. I acknowledge that I'm not good with process and that creates connection. You can get along the best with your peers if you're not in competition with them, and instead you show that you're caring, compassionate, and open. Then it's like two really good friends trying to figure a problem out.

> Sometimes the pressures are intense. I have worked for many leaders who are really smart and really driven. I had to understand what they were trying to achieve and figure out how to get the results my way. But sometimes I lose sight, and when that happens, I lose connection with myself and connection with others. Understanding where people come from helps to understand why they focus on what they focus. I wish I would have taken more psychology courses! Because

I have found that most people are driven by what happened in childhood. I try to focus on relationships because I believe by fixing the relationship, the problem will be solved.

It hit me when you, Michelle, were talking to me about delivering presentations. I think, personality-wise, I tend to be a pleaser. And I was trying to deliver my presentations by acting like what I thought others wanted as opposed to being my natural self. And then when I gave myself permission to be my natural self when presenting, I received so many compliments. People wanted me to be authentic and genuine and true to myself. So then I thought it must be okay to be who you are in your day-to-day life as well. So I've been pretty authentic ever since. And it has paid off tremendously.

"At the end of the day, we are all seeking the same result, which is understanding."

–JIM L. MORA
FORMER HEAD COACH, UCLA, SEATTLE SEAHAWKS, ATLANTA FALCONS

I had the honor of interviewing Jim L. Mora, two-time NFL head football coach and most recently the head coach of UCLA from 2011–2017. Jim is the son of Jim E. Mora, who coached the New Orleans Saints for ten years and took them to their very first playoff game.

I was curious if Jim struggled connecting with himself, considering he grew up with a father who was a successful NFL coach. Did he try to be like his dad, act like his dad, coach like his dad? Did he struggle finding his voice as a football coach?

I never modeled myself after anyone. And even though my dad was a former Marine, he wasn't the Great Santini. He told me to be a continuous lifetime learner: to observe all leaders and learn what works. I would recognize positive traits of the leaders I admired and how they connected with people. I was fortunate to work under football legends like Bill Walsh and Jim Finks. I asked for feedback all the time. I asked them to watch my team meetings and tell me what I could do better. I never asked, "What would you do?" I wanted to be my own person.

My father instilled the belief in me that my standard had to be beyond reproach. If I was demanding perfection from my players, then I had to demand perfection from myself first.

I'll never forget when I was working for the Saints under him as a defensive backs coach. He was sick right before training camp and asked me to bring over my books that I had prepared for my players. I dropped off the books at his house, and he called me shortly after. He said, "You have to type it again." I asked, "Why?" He said, "Because you spelled receivers wrong five times." This was before spell check! He said, "How can you expect your players to pay attention to detail and to be exacting if you can't get it right yourself? Do you expect your players to give 110 percent if you can't get the spelling right?"

This lesson from my father taught me the importance of owning your communication.

Jim knew that he had to create a winning culture. And to do that, he had to hone his communication. Because as he says, "Culture precedes success. Language dictates culture. And leaders control language."

I learned how to take my ego out of my communication. Rather than asking "What were you thinking?" in a critical way, instead I would say, "Tell me what you were thinking" in an inquisitive way. Rather than saying, "Do you understand me?" I would ask, "Am I making myself clear?" Because at the end of the day, we are all seeking the same result, which is understanding. One of my favorite quotes is: "If you step on a man's shoes, make sure you leave a shine." I held the players accountable, I was tough and direct, and I had high expectations, but the players knew that my ego was tied to their success and the team's success. The players knew they could trust me.

"We all have our own communication style. Discover the best method that works for you and learn how to adapt your style to the person you are leading."

–WARNER THOMAS
PRESIDENT AND CEO, OCHSNER HEALTH

I have had the true pleasure of serving as a leadership coach with Ochsner Health since 2015. While working with many of the top leaders in the system, I have had a front-row seat watching Ochsner grow at an exponential rate. Their strategy has been to grow through partnerships and acquisitions. What began in 1947 in a former Army post hospital, Ochsner Health now employs more than thirty thousand employees and more than thirteen hundred physicians in over ninety medical specialties and subspecialties. The system coordinates and provides clinical and hospital patient care across the Gulf South region through its forty owned, managed, and affiliated hospitals and specialty hospitals and more than one hundred health centers and urgent care centers.

Warner Thomas was named president and CEO of Ochsner Health in 2012 after previously serving as president and chief operating officer from 1998–2012. As CEO of Ochsner Health, he oversees Louisiana's largest nonprofit academic health system and its largest private employer.

When I sat down with Warner in his beautiful executive office surrounded by countless awards and recognitions, I asked him when he found his voice. His answer will surprise you.

> Probably only in the last three to five years have I found connection with myself. I've been successful in my career, but maybe in some ways for the wrong reasons. So early on, I was driven by trying to show my parents and others that I could do it, that I could be successful. I was driven more out of frustration, and "I'm going to show you" versus "This is what I want to do, and I want to be successful at it."
>
> And that's why I tell our executives (not just people who work for me; I'm talking about our top two hundred leaders), "All of you are talented. You're accomplished. All of you could go and work as consultants. All of you could go get hired by other organizations. I mean, you've made it! *Now* the question is, What do you want to do? What is it that is going

to drive you? What is it that you want to accomplish?" And I think that's hard work.

Warner strongly encourages his leaders to get a coach if the resources allow for it and partake in the 360° feedback review process. He believes that feedback received from peers is an excellent way to connect with yourself and improve your communication skills.

If you can get a 360° review, if that has been presented to you as an option, to get a coach, do it. Because a lot of people are scared that others are going to notice your blind spots, but they already know them. Feedback is a gift!

Warner and I discussed the idea that how we think about ourselves informs the script that goes through our heads and how that affects how we interact with the world around us:

Everything you look at, you look through the lens of your own world view. So the actual events times your beliefs equals whatever the situation is. I grew up in a small town in Vermont and when we had thunderstorms, it would rain usually at the end of the day when it got really cool at night. So I see a thunderstorm I think, *Oh, kind of cool.*

My daughter grew up here in New Orleans. When she sees thunderstorms, she thinks hurricanes, she thinks Katrina. So when she sees storms she's saying, "Is there a storm coming? Is there a hurricane coming? Like what's going on?" Totally different experience. But it's based on your beliefs and your experiences. So we all kind of look through that lens, and you sometimes realize, "No, it's not really a hurricane; it's just rain," you know?

Warner gave the following checklist of communication characteristics that he believes every good leader must possess:

> I do think you have to have certain characteristics to be a leader. So if you're an introvert and you don't talk to anybody and you can't communicate, you're probably not going to lead the group. But you can be an extrovert and communicate and not be a leader. So I think you've got to have some innate qualities. You have to be a good communicator; you have to be able to connect and build relationships with people. I think you've got to be a good thinker, a longer-range thinker. I think you have to be able to problem solve and deal with adversity and/or conflict. But I think to your point, Michelle, about being connected and comfortable with yourself, ultimately, if you're going to be happy and fulfilled, that's going to be something that has to be sorted out by you.
>
> I think you really have to be willing to learn and to be open and to adapt to be a great leader. Leaders also have to be able to connect with people and have energy and lead with optimism and have that right kind of connection. They have to want the job. They have to want to be here. I don't want people who don't want to be here.
>
> I communicate and lead very differently than Pete November. Different than Mike Hulefeld (chief operating officer of Ochsner Health), different than Tracey Schiro (chief risk and human resources officer of Ochsner Health). So we all have our own styles. You have to find your own style that works for you and how to adapt your style to the person you are leading.

Let me remind you that Warner has been named one of the most influential and successful leaders in healthcare. And yet he has only recently started to feel comfortable in his own skin. So if you are wondering if it's abnormal for leaders to struggle with connection with themselves, it is *not*. It's quite common. You can still become a leader if you struggle with connection. But for you to be the best version of yourself as a leader, you'll need to work on feeling comfortable in your own skin and owning your communication style.

HERE'S WHAT WE'VE LEARNED

Everyone communicates differently. To successfully connect with and motivate your teams, you must: A) understand your strengths and blind spots as a communicator, B) understand your team members' communication styles, and C) adapt accordingly.

REFLECTION AND ACTION

Let's reflect on your personal communication style. Based on the communication assessment you completed:

1. Describe your dominant communication style(s).

2. What are your communication strengths?

3. What are your communication challenges?

4. How can you adapt your presentations/meetings/emails to complement your communication strengths?

5. Think about a person you work with who has the opposite communication style from you. Name two ways that you can adapt to their style.

PART 2

CONNECTING WITH YOUR TEAM

"Successful people become great
leaders when they learn to shift the
focus from themselves to others."
—MARSHALL GOLDSMITH

IN THIS SECTION, you will hear from our fearless leaders about how they successfully connected (or didn't) with their teams. Specifically, you'll learn how to:

1. Show care and compassion for the whole person

2. Listen to lead

3. Act as a servant leader

CHAPTER 4

SHOW CARE AND COMPASSION FOR THE WHOLE PERSON

remember sitting on the gold shag carpeted floor of my father's home office as a child and pulling the book *How to Win Friends and Influence People* by Dale Carnegie off the shelf. I came across a passage from the book that has stuck with me ever since:[11]

When I was five years old, my father bought a little yellow-haired pup for fifty cents. Tippy was my constant companion for five years. Then one tragic night—I shall never forget it—he was killed within ten feet of my head, killed by lightning. Tippy's death was the tragedy of my boyhood.

You never read a book on psychology, Tippy. You didn't need to. You knew by some divine instinct that you can make more friends in two months by becoming genuinely interested in other people than you can in two years by trying to get other

---

11   Dale Carnegie, *How to Win Friends and Influence People* (New York City: Simon & Schuster, 1936).

people interested in you. Let me repeat that. **You can make more friends in two months by becoming interested in other people than you can in two years by trying to get other people interested in you.**

I remember thinking, *Yes, that's exactly right.* You make more friends by showing genuine interest in other people than by trying to get them interested in you. I was in the middle of moving around every two years. I was learning the hard way that you don't make friends in new places by talking about yourself or how great your last city or school or former friends were. You make friends by listening to their stories, learning about and participating in their traditions, and ultimately showing care and compassion toward them as a whole person. You make friends by discovering and emphasizing what you have in common. So even if you're moving from the Northeast to the Deep South, you search for connection and commonality with others.

I was reminded of this lesson most recently when all my classes had to abruptly move from in-person to online during the COVID-19 outbreak. As a private liberal arts university, Loyola prides itself on experiential engagement with the students in small class sizes. I had previously resisted teaching online because my courses (business communication and leadership) are highly interactive with lots of small group exercises and role playing. Despite the awkwardness of suddenly teaching via Zoom, I made the concerted effort to connect with each student individually. I began many classes by asking each student to share how they were feeling about the pandemic, how they were faring emotionally, what they were grateful for, and so on. I tried to find a way to inquire about their lives and experiences. I tried to follow the advice I learned in Dale Carnegie's book: show interest in others in order to connect.

This strategy worked. I recently received an email from my dean at

Loyola University that I won a new award called the Creative Canvas Course Award, which essentially was for the most creative teaching during the crisis. I'll be very honest: I don't think my teaching was particularly creative at all. I'm convinced I received the award because I took the time to listen and connect with each and every student.

Carnegie's lesson also bore out in the pulse checks that I had been conducting with my clients at the same time. During these pulse checks, I would ask questions to uncover the best practices of the new world of working from home. When I asked the question, "What is working well?" the overwhelming response was when their leaders showed care and concern about them as human beings going through a tough time. When I asked the question, "What is not working well?" the answer was when their leaders were only focused on business results. During that time of tremendous stress and anxiety, people needed to be heard and understood if they were going to stay motivated to achieve organizational goals.

Research shows that positive interpersonal connections may lead to the development of characteristics that promote workplace flourishing,[12] and such connections are key predictors of organizational commitment involving increased team performance, effectiveness, and efficiency.[13] Healthy interpersonal connections also boost positive group characteristics including cooperation, teamwork in general, and productive conflict, which contributes to a competitive

---

12   Nicola S. Schutte and Natasha M. Loi, "Connections between Emotional Intelligence and Workplace Flourishing," *Personality and Individual Differences* 66 (August 2014): 134–139, https://doi.org/10.1016/j.paid.2014.03.031.

13   T. C. Reich and M. S. Hershcovis, "Interpersonal Relationships at Work," in *APA Handbooks in Psychology. APA Handbook of Industrial and Organizational Psychology*, ed. S. Zedeck, vol. 3, *Maintaining, Expanding, and Contracting the Organization* (Washington, DC: American Psychological Association, 2011), 223–248.

advantage between organizations.[14]

Meaningful connection with your team is crucial for successful leadership. When your employees don't trust you, you are no longer seen as a leader. And in order to instill trust, you have to make meaningful connections. Leaders must treat their employees with dignity and respect rather than focusing solely on the results that they bring to the organization. When a leader operates from a set of values based on interpersonal kindness, he or she sets the tone for the entire company. In the book *Give and Take*, Wharton Professor Adam Grant demonstrates that a leader's kindness and generosity are strong predictors of team and organizational effectiveness.[15]

In fact, Jeff Weiner, former CEO of LinkedIn, is on a life mission to spread the gospel of compassionate leadership. When Weiner was an executive at Yahoo in 2001, a journalist shadowed him for an article and described Weiner's leadership style as "wielding his fierce intelligence as a blunt instrument."[16] When Weiner read that description, he realized that his leadership style was effective at achieving results but not effective at managing his team. Rather than inspiring, he was shutting people down. So when he became CEO of LinkedIn in 2008, he decided to make compassion the focal point of the entire

---

14   Karen Niven, David Holman, and Peter Totterdell, "How to Win Friendship and Trust by Influencing People's Feelings: An Investigation of Interpersonal Affect Regulation and the Quality of Relationships," *Human Relations* 65, no. 6 (April 30, 2012): 777–805, https://doi.org/10.1177/0018726712439909.

15   Emma Seppälä and Kim Cameron, "Proof That Positive Work Cultures Are More Productive," *Harvard Business Review*, December 1, 2015, https://hbr.org/2015/12/proof-that-positive-work-cultures-are-more-productive.

16   Jeff Weiner, "LinkedIn's Jeff Weiner: How Compassion Builds Better Companies," Knowledge@Wharton, May 17, 2018, https://knowledge.wharton.upenn.edu/article/linkedin-ceo-how-compassion-can-build-a-better-company/.

organization's culture. "Managing compassionately is not just a better way to build a team; it's a better way to build a company."[17]

Weiner believes that compassion is the reason why LinkedIn has achieved unprecedented growth. Under his leadership, LinkedIn has grown from 338 employees to over 16,000, and revenue increased from $78 million to over $7.9 billion.[18] LinkedIn was then acquired by Microsoft in 2016 for $26.2 billion.[19]

Now that we know how important compassion is for connecting with teams, let's learn how our leaders demonstrate care and compassion to their employees. Specifically, we'll hear from John Nickens, Kenneth Polite, and David Callecod.

"To make meaningful connections with your employees, you have to show that you care about them."

–JOHN R. NICKENS IV
CEO, CHILDREN'S HOSPITAL NEW ORLEANS

When John was in his first year as CEO of Children's Hospital, he wanted to know which companies in New Orleans were known for providing excellence. He was trying to figure out creative ways to show employees that he cared about them and valued

---

17   Ibid.

18   Bill Snyder, "Jeff Weiner: Manage Compassionately, and Prepare for the Next Worker Revolution," *Forbes* India, August 29, 2017, https://www.forbesindia.com/article/stanford/jeff-weiner-manage-compassionately-and-prepare-for-the-next-worker-revolution/47945/1.

19   "Microsoft to Acquire LinkedIn," Microsoft News Center, June 13, 2016, https://news.microsoft.com/2016/06/13/microsoft-to-acquire-linkedin/.

their hard work. So he asked 150 leaders to give examples of excellence in the city. Many leaders mentioned the New Orleans Saints, but the majority recommended Commander's Palace, a four-star Louisiana Creole restaurant and world-famous landmark since 1893:

> I went and met with the owners of Commander's Palace, and they shared with me the system they have in place and the signals they have to communicate with all employees, so they can provide an exceptional experience.

> The Commander's Palace Bell of Excellence is our vision for the employee of the month. You can go online and fill out a form to nominate somebody who went above and beyond to be excellent. I take that person to lunch, along with their boss, and I put a Commander's jingle bell around their neck, and they wear it for a month, so everyone knows they are the Bell of Excellence winner.

> In the past two years, I've done this with over fifty employees. And when we're out to lunch, I ask them to tell me their story. I want to know where they grew up, how they got into this occupation, and why Children's Hospital? It gives me a feel for what they truly care about. And then I share my story with them. And what I've learned is that to make meaningful connections with your employees, you have to make time to get to know them as real people. This luncheon provides a wonderful opportunity for connecting one-on-one and showing you care.

"Push the paper aside. It's always gonna be there, but walk the halls of your office and connect with people."

–KENNETH POLITE

ASSISTANT ATTORNEY GENERAL, CRIMINAL
DIVISION, US DEPARTMENT OF JUSTICE

When Kenneth Polite became the US Attorney for the Eastern District of Louisiana in 2013, he entered an office that had recently been plagued by scandal, leading to the eventual resignation of his predecessor. Kenneth discussed the difficulties and the importance of rebuilding morale right away, and he immediately found ways to show care and compassion to his new team.

I ended up inheriting an office where morale was just terrible. I would imagine it was at its lowest point in the history of the office. And it was the first time the office had ever been knocked down as a result of a scandal. And so we had a lot of work to do in order to focus on rebuilding morale, lifting up the people who were there, and refocusing them on the work. My message to them was: "I'm here to take care of you. I'm here to protect you. I'm here to take all the arrows, so that you can concentrate on the work."

So I tried to refocus the office and to lift up the spirits of folks there as much and as quickly as possible. That was essentially job number one. I remember my first speech to the office and talking about my story of applying to that office before, and how this was the group that I wanted to work with all along. And then the next morning I surprised them with a catered breakfast for the whole office. We needed to hang out like a family and eat as we do in New Orleans. And we needed to start rebuilding because there was a lot of distrust among the staff.

The one piece of advice given to me by Attorney General Eric Holder (from 2009 to 2015) that always stuck with me: "Push the paper aside. It's always gonna be there, but walk the halls of your office and connect with people. " And for that office at that time in particular, when our reputation and our credibility were being questioned by so many, we had a lot of work to do to rebuild those connections and those relationships.

Kenneth talked about how he showed care and concern to the external community, which in turn changed the public sentiment about his organization:

External rebuilding was important for the office's reputation. We needed to rebuild, and the only way we could do that uniquely was through connections and through relationships. Face-to-face meetings became a very significant part of the work early on. I would often say to the team: "I've got to spend the whole day at the courthouse. I need to sit down and talk to all the judges, probation, and parole. I need to meet with the heads of the FBI and the DEA." And when I would travel out to the parishes (counties), I would ask to meet with the parish president, the sheriff, and the district attorney. I would ask if I could visit a school and meet with some local business leaders. And I can tell you, each and every visit, I would hear the same thing: "This is the first time we've had the US Attorney come directly to us in our parish." Connecting with those communities by showing care and compassion was essential to the rebuilding process, both internally and externally.

"Learn what makes your employees tick, emphasize it from the very beginning. Start each interaction with a personal conversation so that you learn something new about them."

—DAVID CALLECOD

FORMER PRESIDENT, LAFAYETTE GENERAL HEALTH

From 2008 until 2021 when he retired, David Callecod was the president of Lafayette General Health in Lafayette, Louisiana. During his tenure, David helped grow the organization from two humble facilities to a seven-hospital system with nearly five thousand employees. Under his guidance, Lafayette General received awards such as Modern Healthcare's Best Places to Work and the 2017 Pinnacle of Excellence Award from Press Ganey.

David Callecod believes that it's crucial for leaders to connect with employees at a personal level.

One of the things that I think is unique, and that we do really well here at Lafayette General, is that we learn what makes the employees tick. What are their personal interests? We do it from the very beginning. So we have monthly rounding meetings with leaders and quarterly meetings with all staff. An essential part of the rounding is to begin with a personal conversation that is relevant and salient to that individual so that you learn something new about them. So it will be something like, "Hey, I'm so excited! I saw your son Patrick in the paper the other day! His team won the basketball game. How did he play?" These conversations permeate our culture, and they are that personal connection. I use the monthly meeting model with my senior leaders, CEOs, and their reports, and then their reports use it all the way down to our frontline staff.

In order to keep all of this information in order, David and his leaders and employees use a SurveyMonkey mobile software app developed by the chief engagement officer at Lafayette General. The software has three main objectives. First, it provides leaders with targeted questions to use in rounding. The questions are updated to reflect key drivers of engagement, such as rewards and challenges of their work, process improvement ideas, and safety concerns. Second, they track the voice of their workforce by analyzing the responses to those questions to rapidly prioritize follow-up. Finally, they use it to track rounding compliance and to hold their leaders accountable: "We believe in inspecting what we expect."

If we make a personal connection, we start off with some positive affirmation, and then drill down to what things need to be changed and how we can help. It sets the tone. We also use the same tool system-wide; every leader uses the same process to connect and hold people accountable.

When David connects with his staff, he is honest and up front. When he had to step into the CEO role at a failing hospital early in his career, he told the employees: "I know this is tough; a lot has happened. I recognize that this is a very disruptive time. Look, I'm new. We have a lot of challenges ahead, and I know you're concerned. But we can build something great together." Then, he discussed the successful practices already in place and how they could build upon those successes together. He said, "I don't have all of the answers, and it's not going to happen overnight." He was open and honest. He showed care and concern for their well-being. The result was that the staff trusted him. They knew they could count on him.

HERE'S WHAT WE'VE LEARNED

Rather than focusing solely on results, leaders need to make meaningful connections. How? By showing care and compassion for their staff. By taking the time to get to know their team personally. By learning what makes them tick. By beginning each interaction with a personal conversation to learn something new about them. As Jeff Weiner states, "Managing compassionately is not just a better way to build a team; it's a better way to build a company."

REFLECTION AND ACTION

Now that you've learned about the importance of showing care and compassion to the whole person, please answer the following questions:

1. On a scale of one to ten, how compassionate do you think you are as a leader?

2. On a scale of one to ten, how compassionate would your team evaluate you as a leader?

3. Which leader interview resonated with you and why?

4. What are two strategies you could employ to better demonstrate care and compassion?

5. What are some ways that you can demonstrate dignity and respect for your team, rather than solely focusing on their productivity and results?

CHAPTER 5

LISTEN TO LEAD

O ne of the best strategies to connect with your team is demonstrating that you are listening to their ideas. When leaders are thought of as "good listeners," their employees report feelings of belonging, togetherness, inclusion, and social significance.[20]

I learned firsthand about the importance of listening when I was working for Spectra in the 1990s. The ABC television news program *20/20* called us twice in one year to help them with episodes on listening in the workplace. They wanted to know if we were working with any leaders who were facing potential job termination because of their lack of effective listening skills. We searched far and wide for a client who would agree to go on national television to reveal how their poor listening was jeopardizing their position in the company.

We found an ideal candidate who worked for a utility company in Beaumont, Texas. Sam had received feedback that he didn't listen well to the employees or to the customers. He rarely stopped talking, and not only asked the questions but answered them too. So the

---

20   T. C. Reich and M. S. Hershcovis, "Interpersonal Relationships at Work."

20/20 team flew down to Beaumont and filmed Dr. Larry Barker, Spectra's beloved president, facilitating a meeting between Sam and his team of employees. The camera zoomed in on Sam's bright-red face as each of his employees graded his listening skills with a D or an F, but nothing higher. He looked at his team and asked if they could help him become a better listener. Larry and the team all committed to helping him.

The first step to improving oneself is self-awareness. Participating in the *20/20* episode certainly got Sam's attention. The second step is identifying the behaviors that are not working. For Sam, those negative listening behaviors included interrupting, finishing people's sentences, not asking questions, and demonstrating closed body language. The third step is to work on demonstrating positive listening behaviors including asking for others' opinions, not assuming you have the right answer, leaning in to the person you are speaking with, nodding your head, asking follow-up questions, and displaying open body language.

After allowing time for Sam to work on his listening skills, the *20/20* crew returned to Beaumont for the final filming. I'll never forget the last scene of the interview. The camera zoomed in closely on Sam's face. The reporter asked if he was able to keep his job. Sam said not only did he get to keep his job, but "It's like I love her more." When the reporter asked what he meant by that, Sam said, "Now that I sit and listen to my wife when I come home from work, she said it's like I love her more. Just because I've learned how to sit and really listen." So not only did Sam get to keep his job, but he also got to keep his wife!

My interest in leadership listening didn't stop when I transitioned from working at the consulting firm to teaching at Loyola. In fact, listening became a part of my research stream while working with my colleague, Dr. Kendra Reed. We were interested in how leaders could create positive environments that promote effective listening.

Based on our research, we developed and validated the Team Listening Environment (TLE) scale.[21]

We used the following questions to assess a positive team listening environment:

Other team members:

1. Genuinely wanted to hear my point of view

2. Showed me that they understood what I said

3. Listened to what I had to say

4. Understood me

5. Were attentive to what others had to say

6. Paid attention to me

Once we published the Team Listening Environment scale, we then collected data at various manufacturing facilities to uncover if a positive listening environment could contribute to improved financial outcomes. The results of our research showed that the manufacturing facilities with a positive TLE made more money based on their sales and net income than facilities that didn't have a positive TLE.

So why is it important for you to create an environment in which your team feels listened to? You not only benefit from your employees feeling valued and heard, but you also benefit from improved financial performance.

Now that we know that listening is a crucial leadership skill, let's learn how our fearless leaders listened to connect. Specifically, you will hear from Luke McCown, Boysie Bollinger, Swin Cash, David Callecod, Pete November, John Georges, and Judi Terzotis.

---

21   Michelle Kirtley Johnston, Kendra Reed, and Kate Lawrence, "Team Listening Environment (TLE) Scale: Development and Validation," *International Journal of Business Communication* 48, no. 1 (1973): 3–26, https://doi.org/10.1177/0021943610385655.

"Humility is one of the greatest signs of leadership. Don't allow your ego to be the driving force—instead, listen and value the input from those around you."

–LUKE MCCOWN

QUARTERBACK, NEW ORLEANS SAINTS, 2013-2016

When Greg Bensel, the senior vice president of communications for the New Orleans Saints and the New Orleans Pelicans, recommended that I interview Drew Brees as a model of leadership connection, I couldn't agree more.

In 2006, Drew Brees became the quarterback for the Saints and experienced immediate success in New Orleans, leading the team to their first-ever Super Bowl appearance and win in Super Bowl XLIV. Since joining the Saints, Brees led all NFL quarterbacks in touchdowns, passing yards, and three-hundred-yard games. As of the end of the 2020 NFL season, Brees held the NFL records for career pass completions, career completion percentage, and career passing yards.[22] He is regarded as one of the best passers in NFL history and has been hailed as one of the greatest quarterbacks of all time.

Drew asked that I speak with Luke McCown, who was Drew's longest-serving backup quarterback with the Saints from 2013 to 2016. Luke and Drew spent more time together in the locker room and on the field than with their own family members. Luke had an unparalleled view of Drew's leadership and is a positive example of the benefits of working under an exceptional leader.

---

22 "Drew Brees Reveals His Next Career Move," WBRZ, March 15, 2021, https://www.wbrz.com/news/drew-brees-reveals-his-next-career-move/.

I asked Luke to describe how Drew's listening skills allowed him to connect with his teammates.

Drew is very transparent in stating what his personal goals are and asking for feedback from us: "I want to get better at this now." He's got a lot of different coaches and mentors in his life, but humility is one of the greatest signs of leadership. Drew doesn't allow his ego to be the driving force; instead he listens and values the input from those around him. Be able to look yourself in the face in the mirror and go, "Okay, this isn't good enough. It's got to be better here." Or realize that you're not perfect and understand the flaws that are there; be able to connect with yourself and, in turn, with others.

I think Drew is great at honestly assessing himself as a person and a player at the end of each offseason or before every season. I spent more time with Drew than, outside of my wife, I did with anybody else on the planet. And by the scope of things that we discussed or that came up in conversation just sitting in the meeting rooms, it was apparent that he's, as great as he is, even better of a person, quite honestly, than he is a football player, if that's even possible. But as great as he is, he says, "I can do more. I need to be better at this." I think his humility allowed him to care so much because he didn't think that he was perfect. He listened to those around him and constantly tried to be better.

I personally will never forget the first time I saw Drew Brees as the quarterback of the Saints during the reopening of the Mercedes-Benz Superdome, one year after Hurricane Katrina. You could just feel the electricity in the air. You knew that this team under Drew's leadership was going to be something special.

Within the first few years, I observed Drew connecting in two important ways with the fans and the players. He clearly had been listening to the famous "Who Dat" cheer. If you're a Saints fan, you know the words. Before, you might have heard fans here and there around the Dome and on Bourbon Street saying, "Who Dat," but Drew was the first to use the Who Dat cheer to harness the energy of the crowd in a unified way that had not been done before.

Drew communicated to the media what he wanted the fans to do before the start of every home game. Here's how it worked: The captain of the team, after the coin toss, would walk out to the fifty-yard line and raise his right arm. And when he lowered his arm, all the seventy-eight thousand fans would yell the "Who Dat" cheer three times in a row. It goes like this: "Who Dat? Who Dat? Who Dat Say Dey Gonna Beat Dem Saints!"

I happened to be at that game, and I'll never forget being a part of the seventy-eight thousand fans who got to roar at the top of their lungs "Who Dat" three times right before the kickoff. The crowd went crazy. The noise was deafening. The excitement was palpable. The cheer gave the fans a unified voice; it made them feel like they mattered. Giving the fans an opportunity to show their pride and come together to yell "Who Dat" was an incredible way for Drew to connect with the fans, and for the fans to connect with the team.

Another way that Drew listened to connection was with the

"huddle chant."[23] Drew modeled this pregame huddle chant after the ones he saw while visiting US Marines at Guantanamo Bay in the offseason. This huddle chant became famous when the Saints won the Super Bowl in 2010.

Here is how the team huddle chant goes:

Brees: "One."

Team: "Two."

Brees: "Win."

Team: "For you."

Brees: "Three."

Team: "Four."

Brees: "Win."

Team: "Some more."

Brees: "Five."

Team: "Six."

Brees: "Win."

Team: "For kicks."

Brees: "Seven."

Team: "Eight."

Brees: "Win."

Team: "It's great."

Brees: "Nine."

Team: "Ten."

Brees: "Win."

Team: "Again."

Brees: "Win."

Team: "Again."

---

23   Mike Triplett, "Text from New Orleans Saints QB Drew Brees's Pregame Chant," *The Times-Picayune*, February 11, 2010, updated June 25, 2019, https://www.nola.com/sports/saints/article_427276a7-bc16-5cb3-bd56-0595213fccd7.html.

And the fans then joined in with Brees and the team yelling "win again, win again, win again" until it melted into a general mass of whooping and yelling.

Drew used his adept listening skills to bring the fan-favorite "Who Dat" cheer and the Marines' traditional chant to unify the team with the fans. And it worked. Like magic.

"Listen first. You've got to develop a buy-in so everyone is on the same page, and you do that through listening."

—BOYSIE BOLLINGER
FORMER CHAIRMAN AND CEO, BOLLINGER SHIPYARDS

I was just about to send this manuscript off to the publisher when I was chatting with one of my friends, Sally Forman, who is a book author herself. When she learned that my leadership book was about connection, she asked if I had interviewed Boysie Bollinger. I said no; I had not. She said, "Michelle, you can't publish a book on connection without including Boysie. He's one of the very best connectors that I know!" So I immediately scheduled an interview with Boysie, a truly delightful leader.

Donald T. "Boysie" Bollinger served as chairman and CEO of Bollinger Shipyards, established in 1946 as the largest vessel-repair firm in the Gulf of Mexico. A noted philanthropist, Boysie and his wife Joy contributed the largest-ever individual donation to Audubon Zoo, and the largest-ever private gift to The National WWII Museum, both located in New Orleans. Currently, he serves as the chairman and CEO of Bollinger Enterprises, a single-family investment office headquartered in New Orleans.

I sat down with Boysie to uncover the secrets to his success. The first words out of his mouth were: *"Listen to your employees. Listen to your leaders."*

I think it's almost impossible to be a leader if you're not somewhat of a people person. If you build an organization, you're going to be dealing with other people, and you need to gain their respect. They don't have to like you. But they need to respect your intelligence and leadership capabilities and the direction you want to take them. You've got to develop a buy-in, so everyone is on the same page. And you do that through listening. Listening to your employees, listening to your team leaders.

When connecting with others, don't be dictatorial. I am a little dictatorial, but only on direction, not with process. You need to listen to others to develop the process to move your organization in the right direction. Ask your employees, "How do you think we should do this?" Sometimes they'll have much better ideas than you. And outcomes are much more successful if people have a voice in creating them. Then it's their program, not yours. Plus, if they own the process they'll want it to work. They'll kill themselves to make sure the outcomes are desirable.

Get down on their level. I'd go on the floor of the fabrication facility with the guys doing the work. "You do this every day; tell me what we could do to improve the process to give us a better outcome." You want them to think outside the box at the process level, and sometimes their ideas are really inexpensive. If it's an expensive idea, I'd walk them through how I'm looking at whether we should make the investment. "If we make this investment, how much quality do we improve? How many dollars do we save? Less man hours? Better outcomes?" I can't tell you how much I learned from those on the floor, just making sure that the investments were wise. They start understanding how you look at things. Plus, they appreciate how much you care about what they think.

Employee meetings. After purchasing a company in the mid-1980s that was experiencing some difficult issues, I decided to personally conduct employee listening sessions. I spoke to about 250 people in small groups, and eventually I met with all of them. I'd invite the whole board to these employee meetings. We'd all listen to anything they wanted to bring up. I told them the business was very important to us compared to the previous owner, and that they could ask me any questions they wanted. They had never met with the CEO of the previous owner!

During these listening sessions, I learned about things that I didn't even know were concerns. For example, our business was successful, so I thought our sick leave and paid leave were very good. But the employees started to share other ways of doing things. "Can we have our vacation paid out when we take it?" Simple things that made all the difference to them. "We're required to take vacation one week at a time. Can we take it one day at a time?" If I didn't have the answer immediately, I'd always get back to them once we had researched the impact.

We addressed their concerns. Raises, for example. We heard complaint after complaint that employees wanted a raise, but the supervisor would not give it to them. So we spent two years putting together a career path for every job description. Now they had a blueprint in front of them for how to make more money. It was up to them to improve their skill sets for performance and promotional raises. But we only learned that by interacting with and listening to the employees. You can't learn those things from a book.

Listening to your customers. Listen to your customers to discover what's important to them. Is it schedule? Cost? Quality? One of my customers who I built sixty boats for didn't think he could afford us at first. But I started a dialogue asking what was important to him. Then we figured out how to meet his expectations. He became a customer for life.

Boysie's advice to high-level leaders? Listen first! He said that listening has to be the starting point. Listen to understand what other people are thinking. Explain why you are doing something, why you are making that decision. The chance of getting buy-in is much greater if you explain the why. You can bring them around to your thinking.

"When you're driving culture, all these things matter. It's the details."

−SWIN CASH

VICE PRESIDENT OF BASKETBALL OPERATIONS AND TEAM DEVELOPMENT, NEW ORLEANS PELICANS

Swin has excellent advice for how to connect with others when you are a new leader. She believes in the power of going on a listening tour. After accepting her new position with the Pelicans, she spent a lot of time listening to the basketball players and learned that the "family room" in their arena was terrible. Despite it not being in her job description, she made renovating the family room her first big organizational change:

> When I first arrived at the Pelicans, I went on a listening tour to learn about the current culture. I wasn't even hired for a day, and everybody said, "Our family room is terrible, our family room is terrible; all the families hate it!" And I'm thinking, that's not in my job description technically, but let's go figure it out because it's bothering the players. And that was the first thing on my docket after I came in and listened. I said, "We got you."

> So a family room is an area that every basketball team provides for their players' families, where they can watch their loved ones play the game without having to sit in the stands. Before making any changes, we went through the whole NBA to learn what the best family room experience looked like. We wanted to know what the other teams were

doing. As a result, we are now in the top three when it comes to family room experience in the NBA. The new things we put in place include a nanny room, where we have nannies watch players' children so that the mom can watch the game uninterrupted. We created a wall that is a chalkboard for the kids, and there's catered food and everything. It's a pretty big deal.

Swin also discovered that family day was integral to connecting with the Pelicans players and the overall culture:

To make connections with the players' families, we hosted a family day. Everybody was invited: kids, our PR staff, our front office staff, our equipment guys' families. We had games set out. We had some people making balloon animals. We had the bounce house. So they were going through these activities like it was an adventure. "This is the court, this is where daddy comes to work, this is where mommy comes to work, and I'm getting the opportunity to be here!" Coming from a big family, I understand what it feels like to be included.

Because this goes back to our business. People think those things don't matter, but they matter because of two reasons: How do we retain the players that we have? You have to take care of their families, you have to take care of them, and you have to make sure that things are in place so that they want to be here. And secondly, how do we go out and sell it to the free agents? So we want to be able to say, "We have the best culture." So when you're driving culture, all those things matter. It's the details. Like they say, the proof is in the pudding. Yeah, the proof is in the details! But I never would have known how important things like the family room or family day were to the players unless I spent time on a listening tour.

"It is critical to listen to your employees when you're new, and to take the necessary steps to show them that you've heard them. Sometimes making grand, substantial, or symbolic changes early on in your tenure can be an effective way to demonstrate your commitment to a turnaround."

–DAVID CALLECOD
FORMER PRESIDENT, LAFAYETTE GENERAL HEALTH

D avid tells a wild story about the importance of listening to your employees when you're new and taking the necessary steps to show them that you've heard them. He explained that at every organization he's led, there has been a defining moment where he has either "nuked a policy or nuked a person who did not reflect the standards or live up to the standards." David would make these grand, substantial (yet symbolic) changes early on in his tenure as a way to demonstrate his commitment to the turnaround.

During my first few weeks at one hospital, what I kept hearing was, "Our attendance policy is taking two hours of my day. I have this huge binder in my office, and I'm giving people points for being late; it's the most ridiculous thing in the world." And I found out that the HR director had been in charge of a very large health system previously and then came down to our hospital, which had only nine hundred employees and was a sole community provider. He had implemented the attendance policy that they had there (in a large metropolitan area) because maybe he had invented it, or he was just attached to it.

After I heard this a number of times, I kept asking the department leaders, "Well, do we have an attendance problem?"

They're like, "No, I don't have a lot of late clock-ins or absenteeism."

So I called an all-leader meeting in the courtyard outside of the cafeteria. I instructed all supervisors and above to bring their attendance binders. I didn't tell them why they were there. I asked them to line up and dump their binders into a fifty-five-gallon metal drum ...

So I had only been there a short time, and the staff didn't really know what to think of me yet. After giving a brief speech about accountability and the trust I had in our employees to do the right thing, I asked one of our food service employees to join me at the top of the steps. She had been very vocal about how silly she thought the attendance policy was. She was a great lady, and she had a wonderful personality, but it made her so mad being treated like a child. So I called her up out of the crowd, and I gave her a big bottle of lighter fluid, and she sprayed all the binders with it, and we lit them on fire!

It made a huge impression. Now, did the HR guy like me very much? No, because the policy and procedure were his baby, and so he didn't last very long. He was not a fit for the culture that I was trying to build. But that was a defining moment when the employees realized, "Wow, he really listened to us! Things really are going to change!"

David discusses another example of the importance of listening when you're in a leadership position:

At one hospital, after many one-on-one listening meetings with clinical leaders and physicians, I learned that a director of one of the clinical departments was a problem. She was caustic and mean. She was the roadblock that kept every other department from improving any of their efficiencies because she was so unwilling to listen. She said things like, "I've seen CEOs come and CEOs go, and nothing ever really changes." And she had always been viewed as being untouchable. But I terminated her after she had indicated that she was not going to be a part of any of the changes that we wanted to implement. After that, everyone started complying really quickly.

You not only have to show the employees that you as a leader are listening, but you also have to promote the importance of listening throughout the organization.

"If you can get a group of people working well together and feeling good about working together, they can solve any problem."

—PETE NOVEMBER
EXECUTIVE VICE PRESIDENT AND CHIEF FINANCIAL
OFFICER, OCHSNER HEALTH

P ete's mantra when it comes to connection is to "seek first to understand." He listens to understand what is driving people, so rather than having a factual discussion, he spends more time getting to know how his staff is doing personally. Are they happy or not happy in their lives at work? Typically, when there's a problem, the issue is not really about the actual problem but the relationships surrounding the problem:

> The more you do this, the more you realize it's all about the people and their relationships. And if you get all that right, then you can get anything accomplished. If you can get a group of people working well together and feeling good about working together, they can solve any problem. It's not like I have some magic solution in my office. But that to me is the key, and that requires you to listen and understand.

> I'll give you a specific example. I was facilitating a meeting with my team about a potential delay in a technology rollout. And the conversation got really, really technical about systems. I was looking at the frustration on everybody's faces. And finally one person said, "Look, here's the problem. We're working on this other big project that is out of town. I'm trying to figure out who's going to take care of my kids for the next two weeks because of that other project. I just don't have any people to help you until January."

> After listening to those concerns, another team member said, "Oh, okay, I can wait until January then. I totally understand." You could see that once they were honest about what their real problems were, the solution became obvious.

"We were open, and we listened. And then at the end of the day, we gave a lot of freedom to the employees."

–JOHN GEORGES

OWNER, *THE TIMES-PICAYUNE* AND *THE ADVOCATE*

John Georges discussed how he sought to connect by listening to his employees after *The Advocate* (Baton Rouge) and *The Times-Picayune* (New Orleans) merged.

After I decided to purchase the state's second-oldest and largest newspaper, the best decision I made was to ask Dan Shea, who is now the chairman of Georges Media, to lead the effort for me! Together with his thirty years of experience in newspapers and my thirty years in business, we took on one of the biggest players in newspapers and ultimately won.

Imagine, we were running a one-hundred-year-old, almost national, family-owned grocery distribution business. And we're all of a sudden moving into the new field of newspapers. We know what a newspaper is because we read it every day. So we think we know, but when you get into the organization, you find a lot of really highly talented, highly trained, highly educated individuals. So when there's a change in ownership, they're going to be very suspect of who you are. You need them to trust you.

You know the myths, you already are kind of aware of people's concerns and worries, particularly a new owner of any business and then a new owner that wasn't *in* the business. So, all of these characteristics make the acquisition even more complex. And we had to introduce a whole new leadership team, who came from a different model, a different city. We can be very tribal in Louisiana with a lot of local pride in different cities. In New Orleans, people like Popeyes and the Saints, whereas in Baton Rouge they like Raising Cane's and LSU.

So we had to connect. We had to recognize those differences. We needed them to trust us, the new owners. So we rolled in taco trucks and hot dog trucks to create a casual environment on the day of the official announcement. We were open, and we listened. And then we introduced the new leadership team. This team had to be qualified and smart to earn their respect.

And then at the end of the day, we gave a lot of freedom to the employees. When I asked the reporters what's different between our style and the others', they said they were able to actually write about what they gathered and what they learned. It's listening, giving freedom, respecting.

We also made a concerted effort to put people in the right positions for them to excel. So if someone's really good at one thing, and really bad at another, you want them to do the one thing they're good at and not the other. This intentional placement allows them to perform better, and ultimately to be happier in their role. You just have to listen and demonstrate respect.

"How can I support you? How can I break down barriers? Let me be your dragon slayer."

—JUDI TERZOTIS

PUBLISHER AND PRESIDENT, *THE TIMES-PICAYUNE* AND *THE ADVOCATE*

In 2018, John Georges hired Judi Terzotis, who, along with Dan Shea, ended up playing a lead role in combining *The Advocate*, *The Times-Picayune*, and NOLA.com into one large media conglomerate. Judi is now the president and publisher, overseeing over four hundred employees.

Before joining *The Times-Picayune|The New Orleans Advocate*, Judi was a veteran media executive who worked for twenty-five years for Gannett, the nation's largest newspaper company. Judi said that she was very fortunate at Gannett to receive a lot of leadership development opportunities. She completed many assessments, leadership profiles, and 360°s, which allowed her to understand her strengths and blind spots. And she learned that many leaders put their heads down and only focus on budget and numbers, and they stay in their corner office and never get out. She said she realized right off the bat that she needed to get out and listen to the people.

> I was very fortunate to have worked for Gannett for twenty-five years. They moved me up very quickly. I went to Fort Collins, Colorado, and it was underperforming, always toward the bottom, and the head of Gannett said to me, "I just don't understand it; we're in a really great market. You gotta go figure it out." I spent the first six months going on a lot of listening tours with the team, the frontline people. I'm

a big believer in the frontline; they're the ones who interact with the customers and the readers.

She realized that the frontline employees are the ones with a wealth of vital information, and she wanted to make sure they were being heard.

One of the reasons why Judi sees herself doing really well at the "connection with others" level is that she wanted to make it all about listening to her staff and helping them succeed. And the second her thought process shifted to "How can I support you? How can I break down barriers? Let me be your dragon slayer," then her career took off.

For example, on her listening tours, she dis-

LET ME BE YOUR DRAGON SLAYER.

covered that people in Fort Collins, Colorado, love their dogs and bring them everywhere. So she created a "Fido Friday" with approval from HR, when employees could bring their dogs to work one day a week. Those Fido Fridays became a hit, but she never would have uncovered the puppy love unless she had gone on those listening tours.

Eventually, Fort Collins became the number one newspaper in the country. *How? Because the team needed someone to not only listen but to believe in them.*

Judi applied what she learned about the importance of listening at Gannett to her new role at *The Times-Picayune|The New Orleans Advocate*. One of the first ways she demonstrated her openness to listen was to start a "Coffee with the Publisher" event once a month on Wednesdays. The invitation to her staff says: "You can ask me anything."

Besides monthly "Coffee with the Publisher" events and town hall meetings, she "rounds" every Friday afternoon. Judi will go around and spend the afternoon just chit-chatting and getting to know her employees and their families and what's going on in their lives. She said in the beginning there was some resistance. People were like, "Oh god, here comes Judi!" and they'd put their head down because they didn't feel comfortable opening up. But now she said it's great, and her staff says, "Judi! Let me tell you about how my grandson won his baseball game. Look at the pictures!"

Through the Friday afternoon "roundings," the listening tours, "Coffee with the Publisher," and town halls, Judi believes that listening, listening, listening is how you effectively connect with others and build trust.

HERE'S WHAT WE'VE LEARNED

We've learned that leaders shouldn't allow their egos to be their driving force. Instead, they should listen to and ask for input from those around them, especially from their frontline employees. When leaders are viewed as "good listeners," their employees report feelings of belonging, inclusion, and social significance. When leaders create an environment in which their teams feel listened to, the overall organization experiences improved financial performance.

Leaders can improve their listening skills by: 1) identifying any negative listening behaviors like interrupting, finishing people's sentences, not asking questions, and demonstrating closed body language; and then 2) demonstrating positive listening behaviors like leaning in to the person you are speaking with, nodding your head, asking for their input and opinion, asking follow-up questions, and displaying open body language.

REFLECTION AND ACTION

1. On a scale of one to ten, how well do you think you listen?

2. On a scale of one to ten, how would your employees evaluate your listening skills?

3. What could you do to demonstrate more effective listening skills?

4. Have you created a positive team listening environment?

5. What could you do to improve the listening environment for your team?

CHAPTER 6

ACT AS A SERVANT LEADER

W e've talked about the negative effects when a leader's quest for perfection creates a culture of fear for employees. When I interview people who had to work under that type of leader, they tell me that there's competition between team members, there's fear of retaliation, and there's overall low morale.

The opposite of that corrosive leadership style is called servant leadership. Servant leadership is based on helping others succeed. Rather than viewing yourself as the all-powerful leader in the highest position at the top of the organizational chart, you see yourself at the bottom of the chart in charge of lifting everyone else up. You see yourself as a facilitator of your team's success. Your mantra becomes "What can I do to develop my people, guide my people, eliminate the barriers in their way, and provide the resources they need to succeed?" The chiefs I work with want their leaders to demonstrate the characteristics of servant leadership: to show empathy, to foster collaboration and build community, to demonstrate respect, to be transparent and honest.

As a servant leader, you are a "servant first" and a leader second—

you focus on the needs of others, especially team members, before you consider your own needs. You acknowledge other people's perspectives, give them the support they need to meet their work and personal goals, involve them in decisions where appropriate, and build a sense of community within your team. Research demonstrates that this other-centered orientation leads to higher employee engagement and job performance, increased innovation and creativity, and stronger and more trusting relationships with team members and other stakeholders.[24]

I call this approach "the leader as the coach." I spend most of my time these days helping leaders create environments where their employees feel safe and comfortable to ask questions, take risks, and make mistakes and not be shamed for it. Research shows that employees who feel safe enough to take risks innovate more, turning new ideas into more effective business processes, resulting in increased revenue and profit.[25]

Now that you understand why servant leadership is crucial to an organization's success, let's hear how our leaders incorporate servant actions within their companies. Specifically, you will hear from Larry Closs, Pete November, Luke McCown, and Warner Thomas.

---

24 Robert C. Liden, Sandy J. Wayne, Chenwei Liao, and Jeremy D. Meuser, "Servant Leadership and Serving Culture: Influence on Individual and Unit Performance," *Academy of Management Journal* 57, no. 5 (October 15, 2013), https://doi.org/10.5465/amj.2013.0034.

25 Seppälä and Cameron, "Proof That Positive Work Cultures Are More Productive."

"As a servant leader, you're just trying to provide support and guidance. Part of that process is to provide space for them to grow and make mistakes. No different than a parent."

–LARRY CLOSS
CEO, MAXHOME

---

had the honor of serving as Larry Closs's coach in 2019. Larry is a driven, creative leader who achieved significant success with the company he founded, MaxHome. MaxHome specializes in bathroom remodeling, windows, and outdoor living. After starting his business in New Orleans in 2002, Larry faced enormous challenges when Hurricane Katrina destroyed his entire stock in 2005. Undeterred, Larry opened a new warehouse fifty yards away and reevaluated his business model to offer a bigger range of products and services. MaxHome is now one of the fastest-growing home improvement companies in the county—*Inc. Magazine* awarded MaxHome the number one fastest-growing contractor in America—and the fifty-second fastest-growing company overall.

Larry believes that his best leadership practice is connection with his team. He feels that he does a good job with authenticity but recognized early on that he had an aggressive "Type A" personality. He grew up on the east coast and learned as a child on the football field that if he took responsibility and apologized for his mistakes, it helped him connect with others. Then once he learned more about leadership, he realized that vulnerability and fallibility connected him to others because "You never want others to think that you're perfect. If you show your imperfections, people will help you."

Larry worked in high-grossing situations while he was getting his businesses off the ground. At a certain point, he realized that he needed to be more of a collaborator and servant leader. Larry's big wake-up call occurred when he had a daughter. He realized when she was little that his demanding "Type A" style wasn't a good way to parent. He understood that his "Type A" personality caused mental stress on himself and others, and he recognized that he had to change as a person in order to affect leadership change. Larry believed that the traits that got him to midlevel would not get him to the next step up the ladder. He believed that his "Type A" personality stifled safety, and that his leaders didn't feel safe around him.

Now, Larry has a more servant-based leadership style. He and his managers have "Gratitude Meetings," where they read aloud what they're grateful for and how they messed up. Before the meeting, they document the things they've accomplished so that others can read them, but the most important aspect of this meeting is showing gratitude and fallibility.

Larry doesn't lead all the meetings anymore because he's busy growing other people. Now, his philosophy is: "I'm here to help you." Larry says that he didn't exactly go "from Type A to Buddhist Zen," but that it's a journey and not a destination.

> They're thankful now, because the way I'm doing things is to help them. And I have specific tools that they don't have, but I'm being very, very cautious about it. For example, I went over the top today to tell a woman that I'm meeting with— who is two levels under me—"Look, I'm here to try to help you; don't worry about this."
>
> When you have an "A personality," you drive, drive, drive and want to get shit done. You are used to demanding results.

But as a servant leader, you're sitting back and just trying to provide support and guidance and helping them navigate. Part of that process is to provide space for them to make mistakes. You have to provide space for them to grow. No different than a parent.

"To create an environment where you can take chances and risks and accomplish long-term goals, you have to get things done in a way where your staff feels safe and comfortable and trusted and supported. Oftentimes, how you get something done is more important than what you get done."

–PETE NOVEMBER
EXECUTIVE VICE PRESIDENT AND CHIEF FINANCIAL OFFICER, OCHSNER HEALTH

Pete believes that the best leaders have a servant leadership mentality. Pete said:

How you get something done is more important than *what* you get done. And a lot of people think, as leaders, just as long as goals are being accomplished, and there are great results, you're going to keep advancing. But the truth is there's a limit to that. To get things done long-term, and to get to a place where you can move at the pace you want to move, and where you can create an environment where you can take chances and risks, you have to get things done in a way where people feel safe and comfortable and trusted and supported. And if they don't feel all that, then the results will come, but it'll be short-term.

Pete relayed a story of working in a law firm under his first mentor:

One partner was the kindest, sweetest, most authentic man who supported me wholeheartedly. I felt like he was my father. Now, he was also really smart. And he expected me to work really hard and to get a lot of stuff done and had really high expectations. But I knew I could trust him, and he cared about me, he was a gentleman, and he showed compassion. I would have walked through fire for him and said, "Thank you. Can I do it again?"

I contrast that with another partner who was really, *really* smart and really, *really* driven, but not a compassionate and trusting person. Someone who you felt like if you made a mistake, there were consequences. And there wasn't a personal connection. One of my proudest moments at the firm was the day our managing partner asked this very smart and profitable partner to move to another firm because he did not represent the culture the firm expected. That was one of the great leadership lessons and examples of my career. Culture took precedence over results.

Pete continued:

I have seen many people throughout my career who are hard chargers who get a lot of stuff done. But you know, their people don't enjoy working with them. And it's because they don't feel supported or cared for. Instead, it's all about measuring the results and showing the accountability and not the personal, caring side. And again, every case I've ever seen, it works for a short period of time. But it's not sustainable.

For years I thought, *Well, I can try to build processes and systems to help make bad leaders successful.* But what I've learned is you could build all the processes and systems, but at the end of the day, if you've got someone who's not a good leader, it doesn't work. But when I changed out the leader, everything magically flourished. Because it all ties back to the leader, not the processes or the systems.

It's similar to parenting. I mean, what makes a good parent? The child knows that mom or dad is always gonna support them and cares about their well-being. They will be there no matter what, when they make mistakes, in good times and bad. But good parents also want their kids to achieve and be successful. And so the child works hard to make their parents proud of them, because they know that their parents love and support them.

"Have your team members set personal goals for themselves and memorize their goals. Use your experience and talent as a leader to help them better their skills so that they can feel accomplished and valuable to the organization."

–LUKE MCCOWN

QUARTERBACK, NEW ORLEANS SAINTS, 2013-2016

D rew Brees is a great example of someone who truly connects with his teammates. I asked Luke McCown to talk with me about how Drew uses servant leadership to develop the players around him.

When we started our offseason throwing program, Drew would lead meetings and say, "Here are three things that I'm working on. And I need you guys to help me. These are personal goals and team goals." And then he would go to each individual player, whether it was Devery Henderson or Marques Colston or Pierre Thomas, or a player who was a long shot to make the team. But he would go to those players and say, "I need each of you to give me three goals, personally, that you want to achieve, things that you want to work on, and then three goals for the team." Drew actually went and memorized those goals. He memorized everybody's personal goals that they set for themselves.

And the whole premise behind that was: "I want to help them reach their goals. I want to use what I've achieved to better their talent or their craft, so that they have an opportunity to extend their career." And I took away how deeply Drew cared about everybody on that team.

Drew knew their names and wanted to know their background. It was really remarkable to see how much he cared. That was probably the first thing that stood out to me. Here's this guy who is a future Hall of Famer trying to win another Super Bowl. And yet, it certainly seems like the most important thing to him is watching these players around him achieve their goals, even more than him achieving his own goals. And it stood out to me that if you don't truly *care* about the guys who you're leading, then you're not a true leader.

Drew's a very busy guy. He only has so many hours in the day to do all the things that he does: study, take care of his body, business ventures, family. But watching him pull these young athletes aside and coach them on how to better accomplish a route after we've had our workout and saying, "Hey, let's work on that. I know this is a personal goal that you wrote down that you wanted to get better at by the end of the offseason." Drew showed that he cared by spending that extra time.

And again, he does this whether you are All-Pro or on the practice squad. Drew's taking the time to help them better their craft. He obviously sees it from the team's perspective: "If *you're* better then it's going to help *me* be better, and if I'm better, we're all better, and if we're all better, we *win* better." But you can't do that unless you care about the things that player number fifty-three on the roster struggles with. I didn't see anybody else during my thirteen-year career do that better than Drew.

I've always desired to walk humbly and place others before myself. But I played in the league for thirteen years as a backup, and I was always trying to propel myself forward to a starting position. I don't know that I felt focused on caring about everybody else's opportunity in the same way that I cared about *my* opportunity because I was always trying to take the next step myself. But realizing, "Hey, here's an elite NFL quarterback who's taking the time to make sure that player X feels valued." And that value doesn't just have to be between September and January. That value can be added to our team through his presence in June and July and March and April and in organized team activities and training camp and everything else. That particular player may not be here in the fall, but he adds value to the organization right now because he's out here working with us to be better. And that effort makes us better as a whole.

"If you can't be 100 percent devoted to someone's success, then they shouldn't be on your team."

—WARNER THOMAS
CEO, OCHSNER HEALTH

Warner Thomas believes that once you've successfully connected with yourself and become comfortable in your own skin as a leader, then you can truly achieve connection with others. He feels that you need to be committed to the people on your team and to their development and success, a necessary component of servant leadership. And it goes both ways. You need to know that the people on your team are committed to you and the organization.

Warner goes on to say:

> The way I think about connection with others is that if you can't be 100 percent devoted to someone's success, and to someone personally who works for you, then they shouldn't be on your team.
>
> And similarly, if those people are not 100 percent devoted to *your* success, it's hard for you to be committed to them. I had someone who worked for me for five or six years, and he was a really smart guy, great knowledge, but he didn't connect with others and didn't connect with me. I really never knew where he was. Was he committed to my success or to the organization's success? I didn't know. But I did know that he was committed to his *own* success. But it was interesting that there was always a wall there. There was no authenticity and no openness. To your point, Michelle, if you can't be open and vulnerable, you can't connect with people. And it's hard to be open and vulnerable if you're not confident in yourself and who you are.
>
> I think connection with others is also about trust. You know the Stephen [M. R.] Covey book *The Speed of Trust*?[26] He talks about "higher trust equals faster speed." And the thing he states in his book, which was really interesting, is pre-9/11, we had a lot of trust. We all just walked down to the airport gates with our families. Everything was fine; there were no

---

26 Stephen M. R. Covey, *The Speed of Trust: The One Thing That Changes Everything* (New York: Free Press, 2008).

issues. So now you're going through security where you have to take off your shoes and jacket, take your stuff out of your bag, because our trust is so much lower. Things take so much more time. And I think that's a really interesting example that everybody can understand. Low trust creates more checking and less speed. True connection with others takes trust and time.

HERE'S WHAT WE'VE LEARNED

S ervant leadership is based on helping others succeed. Servant leaders envision themselves at the bottom of the organizational chart, facilitating their team's success. They see themselves as "servants first" and leaders second. They acknowledge their staff's perspectives, give them the support they need to meet their professional and personal goals, involve them in decisions where appropriate, and build a sense of community within their teams. Servant leaders show empathy, foster collaboration, demonstrate respect, and offer transparency. Adopting a servant leadership style leads to higher employee engagement, higher job performance, stronger and more trusting relationships with team members and other stakeholders, and increased innovation and creativity.

REFLECTION AND ACTION

Now that you've heard from our leaders about how they act as a servant leader, please reflect and answer the following questions:

1. On a scale from one to ten, how would you evaluate your servant leadership skills?

2. On a scale from one to ten, how would your employees evaluate you on servant leadership?

3. Which leader would you like to emulate in his/her servant leadership style? Why?

4. Which strategies could you employ to demonstrate more servant leadership?

5. How can you create an environment in which your staff feels comfortable to ask questions, take risks, and make mistakes?

PART 3

CONNECTING WITH YOUR ORGANIZATION

"If you don't truly believe that culture is very important, and if you don't actually live it and enforce it, then all the other crap is worthless."

–LARRY CLOSS

IN THIS NEXT SECTION, you will hear from our fearless leaders about how they successfully connected (or didn't) with their own organizations. Specifically, you'll learn how to:

1. Personally align with your organization

2. Create a positive culture

3. Own your calendar

CHAPTER 7

PERSONALLY ALIGN WITH YOUR ORGANIZATION

I have heard from many of the leaders who I've worked with that there were times in their careers that they had to switch companies. They had joined an organization because of the job opportunity but eventually realized that their personal goals or values didn't align with the company's goals and values.

Connection with the organization begins with aligning yourself with the organization's mission, vision, and values. You have to make sure you're in a place where you feel your strengths, personality, and style are accepted and where your personal goals and values are similar to that of the organization.

For example, I've been on faculty at Loyola University New Orleans for twenty-one years now, and people often ask me why I've been there for so long, or why I haven't retired to become a full-time executive coach. And the answer is an easy one: because I've believed in Loyola's mission from day one. Even without initially realizing what the mission was, I knew that I had found my home.

As soon as I finished my PhD coursework at LSU, I moved back to New Orleans to complete my dissertation. In addition to writing my dissertation on the weekends and consulting for Spectra during the weekdays, I was an adjunct professor at multiple universities on weeknights. I look back and honestly don't know how I had the energy to do all those things. But I remember loving that time in my life.

In the span of a few years, I had taught at five different universities. And I knew in my heart that if I were ever offered a job at Loyola, that's where I wanted to be. The campus was small and intimate, the faculty and staff were friendly, and the culture was welcoming. Teaching didn't feel like work when I was in the classroom because the students were respectful and kind. They came from all walks of life, from all socio-economic classes, from all over North and South America, with significant Hispanic and African American communities. That diversity brought richer classroom discussion. Plus, they accepted differences among each other, not only in thought but in the way that they looked, whether it was the color of their hair, whether they were tattooed or not tattooed, had piercings or no piercings, participated in Greek life or athletics, or none of the above. I had not experienced that level of acceptance anywhere before, and I cherished it.

Fast-forward to a year later, I was called into the office of the dean of the college of business, Pat O'Brien. (Yes, it's true that our dean had the same name as one of the most famous bars in the French Quarter.) Dean O'Brien wanted to make the course that I was teaching, Business Communication 101, a mandatory part of the core business curriculum for freshman year. So he offered me a full-time faculty member position, and I said, "Absolutely!"

I have flourished at Loyola despite the ups and downs of enrollment and budget constraints because its values of education of the whole person and celebration of individuality and diversity aligned with my personal value system. I'm there because I feel dedicated to the mission, and I get so much satisfaction from helping the students become the best versions of themselves.

Connection with the organization consists of aligning yourself *and* the people in the organization with the company's mission, values, and vision. Let's hear from Juan Martin, David Callecod, Kenneth Polite, Todd Graves, Tania Tetlow, John Nickens, Luke McCown, and Jim L. Mora.

"Taking on the new venture of KIND snacks was a beautiful alignment between my own personal values and the founder's values."

–JUAN MARTIN

GLOBAL PRESIDENT, KIND SNACKS AND NATURE'S BAKERY

Juan started with Mars seventeen years ago as a sales director, then climbed his way up to general manager, then regional president, to global president. Grant Reid, the CEO and president at Mars chose Juan to lead the brand that "represented kindness" based on Juan's lengthy experience, solid values, and compassionate personality.

I asked Juan how he segued from pet care, food, chocolate, and chewing gum to running a new partnership for Mars.

I was running the entire Mars portfolio in fifty-two countries: thirty-three countries in Europe and nineteen countries in Africa. It was a multibillion dollar business, thousands of employees. And the CEO of Mars, Grant Reid, called me and said, "Have you read about our strategic partnership with KIND Snacks?" But I was based out of Europe and Africa, and there weren't any KIND bars in Europe. I had not even tasted the product. Grant said, "I would love for you to run this new business for me."

Grant recognized that I was not the typical leader. I am not a traditional executive. I care as much about the "how" as the "what." I prioritize my time with people I like and care for, because I care more about meaningful connections with others. I don't care about titles. If I had wanted to make the right decision for my short-term career success, I would have taken another position. That's a no brainer. And don't get me wrong; I'm very driven and very competitive, but not at all costs.

When I met Daniel Lubetzky, the KIND founder, he shared an incredible story with me. Daniel told me about his father's experience as a Holocaust survivor, and that he had survived thanks to others' kindness, even from some Nazi soldiers. These experiences reminded him that he was a human being and that there was kindness even in darkness. And based on his father's experience, Daniel wanted to build bridges across people and bring the power of kindness through healthy eating. And I fell in love with this vision and felt a deep connection between our personal values.

So in the end, I decided to take this nontraditional path in order to gain the experiences of working in partnership with a founder, working closely with start-ups and high-growth small ventures, getting exposed to great leaders in the United States, and giving my own family a very different cultural experience. Grant captured it really well when he said to me that he thought this new venture would be a better fit for me, for us, and for KIND.

"When you have a strong connection with yourself, you will end up in organizations that are aligned with your own personal mission. Be true to your personal values, always."

–DAVID CALLECOD
PRESIDENT, LAFAYETTE GENERAL HOSPITAL

David talked about the importance of being true to himself when choosing where to work. Early in his career, he served as CEO for fifteen months at a failing hospital. He was able to turn things around, and the hospital went from being ranked last place to ranked first place in patient experience. But David felt as though he lost himself in the process:

The company that owned the hospital told me that it had been put up for sale. I was secretly meeting with interested companies, investment bankers on the weekends. Yet none of the employees knew. But I knew, and it did not feel right.

So as I was in the process of this, I boarded an airplane on September 11, 2001, heading to the corporate office for a meeting, knowing full well that I was going to basically get yelled at and chastised for performance, even though we were for sale and were doing all these great things.

I'm on the plane, and all of a sudden the events of 9/11 unfold, and the pilot announces: "There's been a national emergency. All planes are being grounded, and we're being rerouted to Kansas City." And the big plane we're on imme-diately banks like a fighter jet, and we start going to Kansas City. We were one of the last planes that landed, and when we got to Kansas City, it looked like a parking lot of airplanes.

And so when I was on that plane, I said to myself, "I love what we've done, but I absolutely hate what I'm doing. I hate it." So the morning after 9/11, I called my boss and I said, "I'm not doing this anymore. I don't care where you send me. If you want me to stay in the company, fine, but I can't do this anymore."

Fortunately, I was moved very quickly to a different hospital, still working for the same company. After arriving there, I was able to use the same leadership process to develop similar behavioral and service standards. This effort led to an increase in operating performance and an improved patient experience. In fact, we became one of the top-performing hospitals in the country! Unfortunately, the parent company was having all kinds of financial issues in other parts of the country and was under scrutiny from CMS (Centers for Medicare & Medicaid Services). They decided to put that hospital up for sale too. I made a decision at that time, as soon as they told me, to say, "Look, I'm out." I immediately started interviewing at not-for-profit hospitals, which I knew would better align with my value system.

David needed to work with an organization that was not out to just make money, make cuts, and sell. He discovered that nonprofit hospitals were more aligned with his values and what he believed in. He knew he could be himself in an environment where the main mission was to save and improve people's lives. David's story is an excellent example of how leaders need to feel good about how they fit in with the organization's overall mission and strategic vision.

"What I was trying to do, through my own personal narrative and values, was to shift the priorities of the institution."

–KENNETH POLITE
ASSISTANT ATTORNEY GENERAL, CRIMINAL DIVISION, US DEPARTMENT OF JUSTICE

Kenneth Polite discussed becoming a US Attorney at the young age of thirty-seven, and how his personal history and experiences enabled him to connect with the position and organization.

Serving as a US Attorney in Attorney General Eric Holder's administration was so powerful because it tied directly to concepts of leadership. The position allowed me to use platforms in a way that were not abusive or oppressive but much more constructive. I think being a prosecutor is incredibly influential. You can do a lot by prosecuting a lot of people, particularly by helping victims, and then sometimes reshaping communities. But at the same time the reality for most people is that when they walk into the US Attorney's office, it means that's the end for them. That's the end of their life, the end of their liberty. It will mean disruption for their families, upheaval for their communities. And that scenario plays out over and over again.

When you think about being smart on crime and using prosecution as a tool, it's one of your tools, but it's not your *only* tool. You can use your platform and your resources on the reentry side to help people transition back into our communities. And most importantly, you can help young people not get involved in the criminal justice system by intervening in their lives and steering them in a whole different path. And so that was the spectrum of tools that I embraced wholeheartedly in my capacity as US Attorney.

And the only way to do that is to reimagine the profile of what the US Attorney is. And this is not to cast aspersions on anyone else; I'm talking about the general nature of what the chief prosecutor looks like. Historically, it is someone who people are afraid of. It's someone who is dropping the hammer on people at every turn. It's someone who is trying to lock people up for as long as possible. It's not someone who is connecting with the community through nonprofits.

And so for me as a leader, it became this space where we had to touch upon and utilize all those tools in a way that could be most effective. So when I needed to be tough and talk tough on the enforcement side, I did that. At the same time, and with the same amount of vigor, I was out at schools and connecting with young people, talking about what resources we could make available to them, what a pathway to education looked like, and what it could do for their long-term trajectories.

I think that every US Attorney has their own different personality, but the office itself is always kind of viewed as the bastion of power, right? And that is just the institution. But what I was trying to do, through my own personal narrative and values, was to shift the priorities of the institution. To use the platform, the bully pulpit, and the ability we typically refer to as the "convening power" to solve the community's problems.

"We are constantly working to ensure that our crew is aligned to our vision, mission, core values, and nonnegotiables. Our success is dependent on our crew being aligned to who we are and what we do."

–TODD GRAVES
FOUNDER AND CEO, RAISING CANE'S

Todd Graves is the founder, CEO, and self-described fry cook and cashier of Raising Cane's Chicken Fingers. In twenty-four years, Raising Cane's has grown from a single restaurant outside the North Gates of Louisiana State University to more than five hundred restaurants in twenty-seven states, plus Kuwait, Bahrain, Saudi Arabia, and the United Arab Emirates. Raising Cane's now ranks as one of the fastest-growing restaurant companies in the United States, with annual revenue exceeding $1.5 billion.

Todd has been nationally recognized for his business excellence. He was ranked number twenty-eight in "Top 100 CEOs in the US" by Glassdoor, was an Ernst & Young Entrepreneur of the Year, received the SCORE Award for Outstanding Socially Progressive Business, and was previously voted the Restaurateur of the Year by the Louisiana Restaurant Association. Raising Cane's was the fourth "Most Admired Brand" by Restaurant Business in 2018 and has the "#1 Most Loyal Customers" via the 2018 Consumer Choice Awards by Technomic.

Todd confides that connection with his own organization has been the most difficult level to achieve for him. Todd says that when they've scaled the business, that's when he's really struggled with finding the right C-suite level executives who can connect with the culture of Raising Cane's, who can make good decisions for twenty-five thousand crew members.

I mentioned to him that "perfection equals disconnection," meaning leaders who care more about being perfect and looking perfect often don't connect well with their organizations. Todd found that to be true. Those types of leaders don't fit in with his culture. They're afraid to make and admit mistakes. They don't lead with gratitude and appreciation.

> We've always had great results with our restaurant leaders because they are all about our crew, our customers, and our communities. Where we have had challenges is with some of our C-Suite leaders. We work hard to interview against a corporate mentality and a self-serving notion. When we have people on our team who put their own career or personal agenda first, we have to make tough decisions. When it doesn't work, it's usually because they've been more per-sonal-focused versus organizational-focused. When they aren't intrinsically motivated and they focus on escalating their own career, it's just not a good fit. Generally, these leaders tend to be less collaborative and don't want to admit mistakes. They are easily offended, and they say things like,

"This is my area of expertise. Don't you trust me?" Of course I trust them, but I'm in the details. I've built every part of this business. And making and admitting mistakes is vital when you're a growing company.

We are constantly working to ensure that our crew is aligned to our vision, mission, and core values: our nonnegotiables. We incorporate all these aspects into our communications, meetings, and training sessions. Just last week we had a kickoff meeting live-streamed in five countries to align on our annual plan. Next week, I'm shooting seven videos for our crew. We connect with them on HotSchedules, an app they use to access their schedules. We are working on a "Crewmember" app, and we utilize my social media channels of Instagram, Facebook, and Twitter to reinforce what we are doing in our restaurants and in our communities.

Our success is dependent on our crew being aligned to who we are and what we do.

"The storytelling around your organization has to have narrative, and story, and examples. That's what inspires people to feel ownership."

—TANIA TETLOW
PRESIDENT, LOYOLA UNIVERSITY NEW ORLEANS

As the first lay person to lead Loyola University New Orleans in more than a century, Tetlow faced particular challenges in carrying out the organization's mission when she arrived on campus in 2018. Without the benefit of decades of intense training like her predecessors, her understanding of Jesuit identity came instead from an unconventional source. Her father once served as a Jesuit and left the priesthood to marry her theologian mother. Dinner table conversation revolved around philosophy; her parents spoke in Latin when they didn't want to be understood by the children, and Tania was sung to sleep with Gregorian chant.

As president, she shows her comfort with the five hundred years of Jesuit tradition. She often expresses organizational purpose in the language of Catholic tradition, taking opportunities to teach valuable Jesuit practices like discernment, a form of spiritual decision-making. She also takes the time to translate these into broader ecumenical language and psychological truth. For example, she states that "we care about each other's safety during a pandemic because it is rooted in the lessons of the Gospel, in the traditions of all of the world's great religions, and because it is who we are as a community."

During her twice-a-year convocations, President Tetlow articulates "who we are and what we are to each other." She crafts those organization-wide speeches to be works of art. "The storytelling around who we are, it has to have narrative and examples. Because that's what inspires people to feel ownership."

President Tetlow uses presentations as a way to connect with the university and its stakeholders. During her speeches, she demonstrates that she has not only high-level strategic vision but also the kind of data that proves the point. "I need to deliver purpose-driven rhetoric in a clearly competent way that reassures people that I'm in the weeds with them, I know the numbers cold, and I've got an answer for the most detailed of questions." She ensures that she shares enough detail with the audience that they understand the matter at hand and have confidence in her abilities as a leader.

Another way that she connects with the organization is through her school-wide emails. Rather than have a communications staffer write them for her, she crafts all of her own messages to make sure they're in her own voice.

She says, "It is a precious thing to be able to communicate by email, one lost easily when people stop reading them. I refuse to allow emails to go out under my name that are boring. And I write every email in a way that's warm and, if possible, a little bit funny." With purpose and feeling, she builds community. Tania's emails are compassionate, empathic, and quite witty and have become a topic of conversation among many faculty members, students, and their parents.

"I'm not anything special, but I know one thing—I can outwork anyone because my role in the mission is clear. I have purpose."

–JOHN R. NICKENS IV
CEO, CHILDREN'S HOSPITAL

John talked about a moment in which he experienced "immediate clarity" about being true to himself and his purpose:

My career was developing, and I felt successful for my midtwenties, but I wanted to grow faster. I had a family with three daughters and felt the stress of building a future. I worked for a demanding, brilliant physician leader, Dr. Ralph Feigin. He encouraged me to be aggressive as a businessman and to deliver the funding needed, as I was the leader of billing and collections for his department.

One day I'm explaining why I can't get a certain insurance company to pay claims on time and basically making excuses. My statement of "I don't think we can hit our goals" infuriates him, and he grabs me by the arm and says, "Come on." We arrive in the Neonatal ICU where you have all these little babies fighting for their lives. We go over to one of them, and he grabs my wedding ring off my finger, and he puts it around the wrist of one of the babies. And he says, "You see how small this child is? Anywhere else other than a children's hospital, this baby dies. Rural hospital? This baby dies. But here, we have the dedicated resources. We have the physicians, we have the intellect, we have the equipment. And do you know how I fund all of that? Because you go get my money. Now go get my money."

I'm standing there, crying as I think about my own three daughters. But I had immediate clarity. This is how I make a difference. What's my part in pediatric healthcare? I don't touch patients. I don't have some master academic pedigree. Hell, I got married at seventeen; I'm not anything special. But I know one thing—I can outwork anyone including an insurance company, and I *will* go get that money. This became a life-changing moment of commitment. Am I tired? I would reflect on the babies in NICU and work harder. My role to the mission was clear now—I had purpose.

It became quite the moment in deciding that I wanted to

run a children's hospital. And I knew it was going to take me twenty years to get there. But I've never struggled with what it is that I want to accomplish. Along the way, you get lots of barriers, you get lots of distractions where you could go do this or that, even ponder "Wouldn't it be cool to do that?" But for me, even if I didn't make it to CEO, I was going to make it as far as I could. Because at the end of the day, I knew I had purpose: I wanted to contribute to making that child's life better.

"Every employee should feel that they add value to their team and to the organization. That gives everybody a sense of belonging and a sense of pride."

–LUKE MCCOWN
QUARTERBACK, NEW ORLEANS SAINTS 2013-2016

The New Orleans Saints and its leadership team, including Drew Brees, created an organizational culture that made sure each player who wore black and gold felt valued, no matter their position, rank, or salary.

Luke elaborates:

I had the good fortune of playing in a lot of different organizations. And one of the things that was different with the New Orleans Saints was that the one common value was clear and evident from day one: It didn't matter your draft position, it didn't matter if you're a free agent, it didn't matter your salary that year. If you donned the black and gold, you added value to the team and to the organization. And that gave everybody a sense of belonging and a sense of pride and a sense of "There's opportunity here for me, because they tell me I have value in this locker room."

I certainly don't want to put any other organization that I was a part of down because they all had tremendous impacts on my life. But when I left New Orleans, I just didn't know that I wanted to play anywhere else. Because I knew how it was there, and I knew the atmosphere and the environment. And when you walked in the door, you felt like you weren't just a number on a jersey or a dollar sign. You felt like you were a part of something that was meaningful: not just to sharpen my bank account, not just to sharpen my credentials or my trophy case. But to sharpen every man in that locker room, everyone in that organization. Whether it's PR or the coaching staff, the front office or the training staff, you felt like you had value. And it's because of guys like Drew, because of that leadership.

When I asked how Drew Brees successfully connects with the vision of the organization, Luke said:

The ultimate goal never changes, but the vision of how to get there changes every year. Leaders have to have the ability to take the temperature of the team and then make adjustments by saying things like, "Hey, that scheme, this type of play, this part of our team didn't work well last year." Then they need to articulate and execute a plan.

And I think that one of the great things about Drew is that

he systematically works on his craft, and every offseason he starts over. He would go back to the very basic fundamentals and build it back up. And then the season would come, and he'd play. Then the season would end, and he'd go back to square one, go back to the basic fundamentals, and build it back up. His ability to visualize—not where we wanted to go because everyone is pushing for a Super Bowl Championship, right? So everybody's going in that direction. But Drew's ability to trim the fat in terms of the things that were unnecessary, then get laser focused and say, "Okay, here's the vision, here's how we get there," was incredible.

I think top down, he and Sean Payton (the head coach) are very like-minded that way. Lots of players have visions, but can you orchestrate and execute a plan that walks out that vision in front of everybody else? Drew did that every year. It stems from Drew's authenticity as a man and his ability to connect with, love, and care about his teammates. Once Drew proved that he was authentic and caring and loving to the "least" of the team, then you believed, "He's got our best interest in mind. He's got a plan and a role for me to play in this vision. So I'm jumping on board."

Drew's ability to lay out a vision and shared values for the team was remarkable! This foundation of leadership started with understanding who he was and being authentic as a man and then caring for his teammates. And once everybody felt cared for, loved, and valued, he cast the vision in front of them, and they followed.

"If you allow yourself to become too focused on yourself, you will lose connection with your organization."

–JIM L. MORA

FORMER HEAD COACH, UCLA, SEATTLE SEAHAWKS, ATLANTA FALCONS

When you fall out of alignment with your organization, it does not bode well. You can't lose sight that, as a leader, you are an ambassador for that brand. You need to be able to model the way and demonstrate leadership behaviors that represent the company as a whole.

Now you will hear an example of organizational disconnection from Jim Mora, when he was head coach of the Atlanta Falcons.

When I was the head coach of the Atlanta Falcons, I went on a radio show in Seattle with my best friend and former college roommate. We were having a great time with each other. The radio host asked if I would ever be interested in the head coaching job at the University of Washington. [Jim attended the University of Washington and played football for the Huskies.] I was joking around and said if the Huskies job ever became available, it would be my dream job. I didn't think anything more about it because I thought we were all just having fun. But by the time our plane landed back in Atlanta, the owner of the Falcons called and said that I had sullied the brand. When I addressed my players in the locker room to explain the situation, I could tell they were skeptical. Almost immediately, I was getting shamed nationally and vilified locally. A few nights later we played Monday Night Football in front of eighty-five thousand fans, and they were yelling hateful things at me. I felt horrible. I had let the organization down with an idiotic remark that I never should have made. I had allowed myself to become too focused on me, and I lost connection with the organization. Within weeks, I was fired.

Jim then shared an example of the cost of appearing to lose respect for your organization and the importance of personally owning your failures.

When I was hired to coach the UCLA football team, I was told to blow up the culture. The team had a reputation of being soft, of throwing in the towel and giving up. I was tasked with the job of making the team tougher. I immediately went to work. I established accountability and was demanding. In my circle, in my bubble with the players and coaches, they knew that I cared about them and their successes. They knew that I would do anything to help them. So if I lost my temper, they knew it wasn't my ego. Instead, it was my quest for everyone to live up to high standards and become champions. I wanted to create a winning culture, a tough culture. So the people in my bubble trusted me. I had earned their respect.

But where I went wrong was with the people outside of the bubble. I could get triggered and ticked off. I sometimes came off as abrasive and a bully. That didn't serve me well. I lost sight of the fact that those people outside of my bubble had influence on the decision makers. I think that's one of the reasons why after we lost the USC game in 2017, they decided to let me go. I definitely could have done a better job navigating the dynamics of the organization. I wish I had understood more clearly that I had not earned the respect and trust of those outside of my players and coaches. They viewed my behavior as destructive rather than constructive. Now I realize how important it is to always be thinking about the organization at large, and about how each and every person is important to the team's success.

I'm not afraid to accept responsibility for my failures. A lot of people want to point their fingers at others. If you are going to learn and grow, you have to recognize your part in your failure. I've learned that I need to treat those who I don't directly touch differently. I would also be more patient. I would work hard at this third level of connection, which is connection with your organization. I think I'd be great at that now.

Because at the end of the day, disconnected leaders fail.

HERE'S WHAT WE'VE LEARNED

Connection with the organization begins when you align yourself—your mission, goals, and values—with your organization's values. You incorporate the company's vision, mission, and core values into all your communications, meetings, and training sessions.

When a leader falls out of alignment with their organization, it can have major consequences like loss of trust or loss of the job itself. Leaders can't lose sight that they are ambassadors for their organization. They must be able to model the way and demonstrate behaviors that appropriately represent their company as a whole.

REFLECTION AND ACTION

Now that you've learned how our leaders successfully aligned with their organizations, please answer the following questions:

1. What are your top three personal values?

2. What are your organization's values?

3. Do your personal values align with your organization's values?

4. If they don't align, what could you change?

5. If you could start your own company, what would its values be?

CHAPTER 8
CREATE A POSITIVE CULTURE

I used to get so excited to receive my monthly subscriptions of *Fast Company* and *Fortune* business magazines. In those magazines is where I learned about "The Best Places to Work," "The Best Bosses," "The Most Positive Work Cultures," and "The Most Innovative Companies." In those magazines, I first learned about leaders and change agents like Tom Peters, Richard Branson, Stephen Covey, Herb Kelleher, Larry Ellison, and companies like Zappos, Southwest Airlines, Google, Yahoo, and LinkedIn.

I couldn't wait to teach my students about work environments that were positive, motivating, and sometimes even fun and cool. The command and control model of organizational leadership was outdated and no longer en vogue. The days were over where it was acceptable, especially during my dad's career, to get yelled at or punished for "taking your kids canoeing." (There's a real story there, but no need to share the details. Those leaders were probably just emulating the behaviors they experienced with *their* bosses.)

But thankfully those negative, punitive, shaming organizational environments are now a thing of the past. A large and growing body of research demonstrates that a cut-throat business environment is harmful to productivity over time. In fact, cut-throat organizations incur the following hidden costs: higher healthcare costs, stress-induced disengagement resulting in higher absenteeism, and a lack of loyalty, which causes high turnover.[27] Leaders now have the opportunity to create cultures that motivate and inspire. Leaders get to set the expectations for the desirable or undesirable behaviors. And the good news is that there's not a "one size fits all" or a specific recipe for how to create a positive culture.

What exactly do I mean by culture? Culture consists of the values, beliefs, behaviors, and experiences that make up the organization's environment.[28] Once a company's culture has been defined, every communication, decision, and action should support the cultural beliefs. This includes all human resource mechanisms from recruitment and hiring processes to performance and review systems.[29]

Recently, Harvard published an article citing the benefits of positive work cultures.[30] They identified six essential characteristics of a positive workplace environment:

1. Caring for, being interested in, and maintaining responsibility for colleagues as friends.

2. Providing support for one another, including offering kindness and compassion when others are struggling.

3. Avoiding blame and forgiving mistakes.

---

27   Seppälä and Cameron, "Proof That Positive Work Cultures Are More Productive."

28   Brent Gleeson, "How Important Is Culture Fit For Employee Retention?" *Forbes*, April 3, 2017, https://www.forbes.com/sites/brentgleeson/2017/04/03/how-important-is-culture-fit-for-employee-retention/.

29   Ibid.

30   Seppälä and Cameron, "Proof That Positive Work Cultures Are More Productive."

4. Inspiring one another at work.

5. Emphasizing the meaningfulness of the work.

6. Treating one another with respect, gratitude, trust, and integrity.

Harvard researchers Emma Seppälä and Kim Cameron conclude:[31]

A positive workplace is more successful over time because it increases positive emotions and well-being. This, in turn, improves people's relationships with each other and amplifies their abilities and their creativity. It buffers against negative experiences such as stress, thus improving employees' ability to bounce back from challenges and difficulties while bolstering their health. And it attracts employees, making them more loyal to the leader and to the organization as well as bringing out their best strengths. When organizations develop positive, virtuous cultures, they achieve significantly higher levels of organizational effectiveness—including financial performance, customer satisfaction, productivity, and employee engagement.

Most of my clients are tired of hearing me say, "Culture eats strategy for lunch," inspired by a quip from famous management consultant Peter Drucker. I agree with Mr. Drucker that if **CULTURE EATS STRATEGY FOR LUNCH.** you don't have a winning culture, your strategy is useless. Yet too many leaders think that the majority of their time should be spent on strategy instead of culture.

So let's learn from our fearless leaders how they created positive cultures. Specifically you will hear from Todd Graves, Larry Closs, Boysie Bollinger, David Callecod, Augusto Martinez, and Robért LeBlanc.

---

31   Ibid.

"Have a 'people first' mentality and work hard
to respect, recognize, and reward your staff."

–TODD GRAVES
FOUNDER AND CEO, RAISING CANE'S

Todd discussed how he built a positive culture by showing appreciation and gratitude for his crew every day.

We have a "people first" mentality. In fact, we have an entire "Cane's Love" department whose purpose it is to respect, recognize, and reward our crew.

We close for every major holiday, even the Super Bowl. We host sixty annual crew appreciation picnics and holiday parties. We've sent one hundred thousand cards to crew members for birthdays, anniversaries, Mother's Day, Father's Day, and more. We celebrate anniversaries by giving them hard hats, salmon, and crystal dogs—atypical mementos rooted in our story. We celebrate restaurant birthdays and minor holidays with cakes, candy, gifts, and much more.

Understanding the fry cook and cashier mentality is a huge piece of connecting with our crew. I consider everyone to be fry cooks and cashiers because those are the most important positions at Raising Cane's. So all our company leaders do extensive training in our restaurants. I don't ask our restaurant leaders to do anything I haven't done or wouldn't be willing to do myself!

We practice "positive motivational management" to praise our crew for what they're doing well and to encourage them to grow and improve. From telling them, "Good job on making that toast!" to teaching them the "why" behind how we do things. If I can show our crew that I'm appreciative, it's going to be a positive experience: from "I'm thankful for you" to "Can you please wipe that down?" or "Thank you for taking the trash out to the dumpster!" Positive motivational management is all about finding and recognizing the right things they do.

Todd has created a positive culture by encouraging the staff to have fun and be creative.

Another way I connect with the employees is that we don't take ourselves too seriously. We work hard to make Cane's a fun place to work.

Back in the early days of Cane's, fast-food workers typically wore a polyester shirt and a goofy hat, while our crew could wear a Raising Cane's T-shirt of their choice. We listened to music and had a good time while we worked, which was not the case in most restaurants. These were my peers—I started two years out of college, and so I wanted to have fun while I worked.

Our managers are serving leaders, ensuring that their crew's job is fulfilling and fun. You can hire somebody who's not happy somewhere else where they know their management doesn't care. But then they come to work for us, and they're happy. It's about culture and environment.

"If you do not think that corporate
culture is important, then who cares
what the hell you put in place?"

—LARRY CLOSS

CEO, MAXHOME

When Larry Closs founded MaxHome, his corporate mission was "Everybody Happy." Some of his best practices for connection with the organization include conducting a "Happiness Huddle" two to three times a year. During these huddles, every manager meets with each department and asks two questions: "What can we do to make you happy?" and "What can we do to make customers happy?" The managers listen carefully to each suggestion. This huddle not only leads to great best practice improvements, but it also ensures that everyone feels listened to, and everyone understands the mission of happiness.

Larry organized a "Culture Committee" to organically spread values, beliefs, and behaviors throughout the company. Despite only having 130 employees, he also started "MaxU" to make sure that his staff had the tools, skills, and resources to grow. MaxU teaches three classes per semester—one business course for everyone, one personal course for health and financial management, and a small discussion class for managers. MaxHome also has a "Values Champion" instead of an "Employee of the Month"—where they reward employees who demonstrate and live the organization's values.

Larry is personally involved in the onboarding process. He meets with each new employee to share his personal story, the company's story, where the company is heading, and its culture. This meeting is welcomed by new employees because it helps them understand how important culture is—the CEO is coming to talk to them about it. Additionally, Larry holds monthly breakfasts with the whole company where they come together as an organization to connect personally and *not* discuss business.

Larry sums up what he has learned from working with many leaders:

> If you do not think that corporate culture is important, then who cares what the hell you put in place? If you don't live it as much as possible, the culture that you put in place, it doesn't make a damn bit of difference. That's the hard work. Anyone can have meetings. You can post your culture and values up everywhere. You can have people singing your values every morning. You can have value games; you can evaluate champions, and these are all things that we do. But if you don't truly believe that culture is very important, and if you don't actually live it and enforce it, then all the other crap is worthless.

"Supervisors should communicate with the employees in a way that shows that they are cared about, versus the old 'command and control' style. Have warm and friendly relationships with your employees, not antagonistic ones."

–BOYSIE BOLLINGER
FORMER CHAIRMAN AND CEO, BOLLINGER ENTERPRISES

Boysie discussed creating a culture shift within his organization that led to happier and more engaged employees. He focused on creating a positive culture through better communication.

I was trying to develop a communication program to better talk to employees. I wanted the supervisors to have a warm and friendly relationship with their staff, not an antagonistic one. I wanted the supervisors to talk to the employees in a way that showed that they cared about them versus the old "command and control" style. And then I saw this grandmotherly woman at a conference. Her name was Mildred Ramsey. She was a union worker at a textile factory in the Carolinas who had concluded that the union didn't care about her. So she led a fight to get rid of the union. She told the leaders: "You don't have an HR problem; you have a people problem. Don't try to convince a mother to come into work if her children are sick. Don't try to convince her."

When I heard Mildred give a presentation in person, I knew that I wanted her to teach my supervisors how to communicate. Every leader had to watch her video tapes. It took a number of years, but she successfully changed the whole culture of our business.

In addition to the supervisor training, I wanted to hold meetings with all the employees to personally connect with them. So every year I would meet with the three thousand employees across fourteen different shipyards. These meetings took about six weeks, and I invited my board of directors, which included many of my family members.

During the forty-five-minute meetings, I would first make remarks about the industry and assure them that the company was financially sound and that their jobs were secure. And then I'd open it up for questions. The group size was around ten people per group in the beginning, and then as we grew over the years, the groups grew to 100 to 150 per meeting. The feedback we received was quite positive. The employees would say, "Here's the boss coming here to tell me everything he knows, and I feel like I'm a part of the organization." Participating in these company-wide meetings was an enlightening experience not only for me as the owner but for the board, the family members, and the employees themselves. It was a great way to connect with each other.

"Allow your employees to develop service or behavioral standards that are important to the culture they want to create or maintain, and then wholeheartedly live and support these standards word for word."

–DAVID CALLECOD
PRESIDENT, LAFAYETTE GENERAL HEALTH

One of David Callecod's most successful strategies to connect with an organization as a new leader is by creating an "Employee Task Force" consisting of high performers and known problem solvers. This committee works together to improve the internal culture, improve patient experience, and establish service standards.

David elaborates:

At my first hospital as CEO, I created an employee task force
to really understand what were the challenges that the organization was facing, because whatever they were, I knew I
couldn't solve them alone. I didn't have a lot of experience.
So I empowered this task force, made up of frontline non-
management employees, to define the ten to fifteen service
or behavioral standards that were important to the culture
they wanted to create. The employees came up with them
and then they owned communicating and validating them.
I wholeheartedly lived and supported the standards word
for word as developed by the staff. And in listening to their
voices and showing that I trusted them, I gained their trust
in return.

David attributes cultural transformation success to two factors:
employee empowerment and employee engagement. He continued to
create these task forces when subsequently leading different hospitals:

Every place I have led has worked its way to the top decile in
patient engagement, employee engagement, and physician
engagement at some point during the time I've been there.
And what's been really gratifying is that, even now as we
have acquired new hospitals, and though I'm not the leader
on the ground directly in charge of these organizations,
we've still been able to replicate those results. So that's been
really reaffirming.

At Lafayette General, David formed an employee task force to
redefine the company's culture, which evolved into the organization's
"Journey to Excellence." An important piece of this work is quarterly,

full-day leadership meetings with a focus on leadership development and the hospital's culture. The team also conducts three expos per year: Engagement Expo, Experience Expo, and Efficiency Expo.

> The Employee and Experience Expos are designed to rapidly identify the newest and best employee engagement and patient experience ideas that we are trying throughout the system. The attendees are not leaders. They are staff-level folks who come from all parts of the system to present what they did, how they did it, and how it impacted engagement or experiences. Sometimes they are sharing what worked, and sometimes it's what didn't work. Those valuable learnings can quickly be cascaded across the system. We also have Efficiency Expos that are similarly formatted but focused on cost reduction or revenue-enhancing ideas. All of these expos not only spread best practices but they're also huge networking, learning, and leadership development opportunities for the staff-level employees who not only are presenting but are also taking ownership in terms of what the department has done and can do.

David made sure that he was connected with the Lafayette organization as they grew into a larger system:

> Twelve years later, we won every award you can think of. We have an average daily census that's close to 400 at the main campus, up from 170 in 2008. We're now the Level II trauma center from the Atchafalaya Basin to the Texas border. We went from having two hospitals and a three-parish service area to seven hospitals with significant presence in nine parishes. And the organization has grown from $170 million to over $800 million in annual net patient revenue. Using

the same techniques here that I had used before has led to success on our Journey to Excellence!

"Money is very important, but if it's your company's main goal, and you start cutting costs and investments just for profit, you won't be as successful long-term."

—AUGUSTO MARTINEZ

FOUNDER AND CEO, PARQUESANTO DEL ECUADOR, SA

A ugusto Martinez was introduced to me by my dear friend Betty Stewart Poole. Betty and Augusto became fast friends while attending Tulane University. Augusto then became very close with Betty's father, Frank, and learned about the funeral business that he would eventually start and run in Ecuador. (Frank Stewart was the former CEO of Stewart Enterprises, the second-largest provider of funeral and cemetery services in the United States. The company was publicly traded and listed on NASDAQ.)

After receiving a degree in Management from Tulane University, Augusto started companies in telecom, construction, education, summer camps, charity organizations, and assistance services before founding ParqueSanto del Ecuador, South America in 2008, where he currently serves as the CEO. ParqueSanto is engaged in the provision, marketing, and sale of funeral and burial services such as cremation, columbariums, and niches. ParqueSanto competes in an area with 1.5 million people, and they hold 80 percent of the market share.

Augusto had to make some tough choices early on in his career.

In the first jobs that I had, I didn't believe in the many layers of upper management and corporate structures. I didn't agree with how they were doing things. For example, in one of the jobs I didn't like the food there, so I joined a committee to get better food. In addition, I thought the internal publications for employees were lousy, so I got involved with changing them. But some people (one of them being my boss) didn't like that. They asked, "Why is this guy stepping on other people's toes?" I had just wanted to help with things that weren't working. But I soon realized that was not possible because those companies were hierarchical and rigid, and I wasn't able to make major improvements or contributions outside my department. I thought there was something wrong with me! But I came to the conclusion that those organizations weren't for me. Ultimately, I resigned and became an entrepreneur. I finally understood that I needed to be starting companies and building positive cultures that reflected *my* belief system.

We invest in people and their workspaces to make them feel comfortable. I tell my employees, "When this is over, the only thing people will remember is if we were good people or not." We have to be good to our families, our organizations, and our communities. Money is very important, but if it's your main goal, and you start cutting costs and investments just for profit, you won't be as successful long-term. Your main goal should be to build quality relationships with clients. If you surpass customer expectations, that's the cornerstone of sustainability of business over time.

Augusto realized that working in a fun and creative environment was important to him, so he worked hard to build company cultures that were fun, innovative, and allowed mistakes.

Fun. We believe in people having fun, but in the companies that I have founded (the funeral home and cemetery business), we serve people in some of the toughest moments in their lives. When we were launching our first cemetery, we wanted people to visit us, but we recognized that the worst invitation a potential customer can get in life is to come to visit and tour a cemetery. So we chose to do something really bold and audacious. We sent buses to neighborhoods to pick up our potential clients and give them tours of the cemetery. There was a live comedy with actors and in their script they would explain the different parts of the cemetery. We wanted our guests to have fun! And it was a total success. We compete in a 1.5 million people market, and we have 80 percent of the market share. We dominate the market by servicing the customer in new and interesting ways. People never thought they'd laugh so hard while touring a cemetery!

Allowed to make mistakes. While you should choose your decisions wisely, you should also get comfortable with making mistakes. In thirty years of experience working in Latin America, I see people who were indoctrinated to be ashamed of making mistakes. As a result of this indoctrination, sometimes they then tried to cover up and transfer blame to someone else. I wanted to change this. When I got comfortable with my mistakes, when I took ownership and responsibility when something didn't work, I saw the vast knowledge and experience that I could gain from owning those mistakes. This is an everyday corporate culture challenge with my work peers.... I'm doing and saying wrong things all the time! But I own up to my mistakes, and I hope to be a good role model for my employees.

Innovative. In order to change the way people think about end-of-life care, we've done some crazy things. For example, we have a sports complex for employees and customers. When you make a preadvanced purchase ("preneed") of a cemetery plot or funeral service, you might use that property in fifteen years. So as a service to our customers and to add value, we built a sports complex and a playground for children with ladders and swings. If you're our customer, you can come play soccer, volleyball, and basketball. Patrons who are attending a funeral can leave their children to play in the playground anytime.

In addition, we now have a grief-support department with psychologists and priests. Grieving is a ritual, and attending a funeral can take you from shock and profound despair to deep sadness and finally to acceptance. It's a ritual for healing, and we all need support during that time. In this area, in 2017, we started the first private initiative for suicide awareness and prevention, where we educate the community about the signs and risk factors. We have two radio programs too. It's impossible to measure how successful this initiative or program has been, but we felt it was the right thing to do. Now we're working with service dogs because we've learned that they can have a healing and calming effect on a person during their grief.

One of the reasons that Augusto has been so successful is because of the positive culture that he intentionally built. His employees and his customers have benefited from creative and innovative solutions in what is typically a somber industry.

"We want our team to enjoy themselves every day while learning and being really productive, and we want them to have joyful and balanced lives while doing so."

–ROBÉRT LEBLANC

FOUNDER, CEO, AND CREATIVE DIRECTOR, LEBLANC+SMITH

Robért has spent a significant amount of time making sure that his employees feel important and are well taken care of.

The vision for LeBLANC+SMITH is really clear: to create excellent twenty-first-century Southern hospitality experiences that enable all people to live joyful, balanced, and fulfilling lives and that develop great hospitality leaders. The way that applies to our team is we want to create an environment where people can succeed in hospitality to the tremendous benefit of their personal health, happiness, and relationships. For too long, succeeding in hospitality typically came at a tremendous cost to one's personal health and relationships. The stress, overworking, physical problems, and relationship issues that typically come with careers in hospitality are unacceptable. We want to shift that paradigm. If you work with LeBLANC+SMITH Hospitality Group, we want you to apply your passion to create things that allow us to bring people together and to inspire people. But you must do that while also having great relationships, and the time and energy to pursue those things about which you're passionate in your personal life. That might be music, reading, film, or coaching youth sport. And so that's how that vision applies to our team. We want our team to enjoy themselves every day while learning and being really productive, and we want them to have joyful and balanced lives while doing so.

We discuss our five values during the interview process, and each value applies to our guests and our team members in equal measure.

The first value is "I see you; I love you," which applies to our guests in the sense of everyone's welcome and should feel completely at home at our spots. As for our team members, this means every single person counts equally and is of the utmost importance to our entire team.

The second value that we have is "Be inspiring," which means that every day, try to do something in life that inspires our guests and inspires each other.

The third value that we really believe in is "Do cool shit and stay humble." We hire a bunch of individuals, and we don't hire them so they can be like someone else. We hire them for who they are. And if you know who you are and you're comfortable in your own skin, that's "cool." And staying humble for us means two things. First, be humble and understand that we're here, personally and professionally, because of a lot of people in our lives who have given and continue to give us a lot. We're also here because many guests come to support us, and we don't ever take them for granted. The second aspect of humility is understanding that you can always learn and grow. We talk about it by saying, "We're really proud of who we are, what we've done today, but what can we do to get better next year? What are we going to do?"

The fourth value is "Teach why." If we take the extra ten or fifteen seconds to teach someone something and explain the reason behind it, two things happen. First, you typically only have to explain it once. Secondly, you create a culture of learning whereby the students become the teachers. This value is based on that idea "If you give a person a fish, they eat for a day. If you teach a person to fish, they eat for eternity."

And the last value that we talk about is "Create joy." We think life is too short, no matter how long you live. But if you live it the right way, you should be able to create a little bit of joy for our guests, for each other, and for yourself every single day.

We all commit to living out this vision and these values immediately upon joining LeBLANC+SMITH, and we spend an extraordinary amount of time discussing and reviewing them throughout our normal work weeks. We want to create a positive culture/environment where people can succeed in hospitality to the tremendous benefit of their personal health, happiness, and relationships.

HERE'S WHAT WE'VE LEARNED

Negative and punitive "command and control" organizations are a thing of the past. If an organization doesn't have a winning culture, their strategy is useless. Leaders have the privilege and opportunity to create cultures that motivate and inspire people to do great work. Once a company's culture has been defined, every communication, decision, and action should support the cultural beliefs. Having a positive culture is one of the most important aspects of keeping staff engaged and retaining great employees.

REFLECTION AND ACTION

You've now learned how leaders create positive cultures, so please answer the following questions:

1. On a scale of one to ten, how would you evaluate your current culture?

2. Describe the best organizational culture you've ever worked in.

3. Could you replicate some of those best practices at your current company?

4. What could you do to create a more positive culture?

5. What methods do you use to keep your employees engaged?

CHAPTER 9
OWN YOUR CALENDAR

One of the edicts I share when I coach my leaders is for them to own their calendars. Owning your calendar is the way that you will connect with the various stakeholders in your organization. Some people call this scheduling process a "meeting rhythm," a "communication rhythm," or an "operating rhythm." But whatever you call it, you have to own it, or it will own you.

A Harvard Business School study conducted in 2006 tracked the calendars of twenty-seven top-performing CEOs of publicly traded companies worth on average $1.3 billion. The purpose of the study was to analyze the raw data of actual time allocation and to provide recommendations on how to increase time efficiency. The authors of the study concluded that the most important step to becoming an effective leader is through proper calendar management.[32]

What does effective calendar management look like? Rather than working in a stressful, reactive state of mind, you should proactively

---

32   Tanya Prive, "A Harvard Study Found That 27 Top-Performing CEOs Use These 6 Strategies to Manage Their Time," *Inc.*, August 4, 2019, https://www.inc.com/tanya-prive/a-harvard-study-found-that-27-top-performing-ceos-use-these-6-strategies-to-manage-their-time.html.

think about the following questions:

- Who are the key stakeholders you should be communicating with? Direct reports? Peers? Boss(es)? Skip level? Frontline employees? Customers?

- How often should you meet one on one with your direct reports? Once per week? Twice per month?

- How often should you meet with your team as a whole? Morning huddles? Weekly huddles? Monthly huddles?

- How often should you schedule division-level meetings? Monthly? Quarterly?

- How often should you meet with frontline employees? Monthly? Quarterly?

- How often should you conduct town hall meetings with your entire organization? Quarterly? Annually?

- How often do you need to embed time to strategically think on your own?

- How often do you need to embed time to creatively brainstorm with your team? Work on team strategy?

- Do you need to block your lunch hour from getting booked?

- Should/Could your meetings be thirty minutes instead of sixty minutes?

- Do you need to embed travel time or processing time between meetings?

Warner Thomas of Ochsner Health, Juan Martin of KIND Snacks, and Robért LeBlanc of LeBLANC+SMITH all emphatically believe in leaders owning their calendars. Let's hear more from them.

"The 'operating rhythm' is the foundation of effective leadership, and the idea of connection and rhythm—that's all part of driving culture."

–WARNER THOMAS

CEO, OCHSNER HEALTH

The "operating rhythm" is the foundation of effective leadership. I tell my leaders to own their calendars, or else their calendars are going to own them. Our operating calendar for the year drives our organization. And the more compli-

I TELL MY LEADERS TO OWN THEIR CALENDARS, OR ELSE THEIR CALENDARS ARE GOING TO OWN THEM.

cated you get, the more organized you need to be, and the more simplistic and systematic in how you do things.

I read a lot about how Jack Welch ran General Electric, and there's a lot of things that I admire and some that I don't necessarily buy into. But one of their best practices is their "operating cycle." For example, they have organized and focused strategic planning reviews and talent reviews. They still hold their annual meetings in Boca Raton, Florida, where they kick off their year with top executives. They have their corporate executive council set their strategy for the year. GE has their challenges now, but for a long time that system was really successful.

Another example is Walmart. They have Saturday morning meetings for their top executives, asking things like "What did the week look like?" Similarly, Jamie Dimon, the CEO of JPMorgan Chase, had huddle calls multiple times per day to check in with his organization when the whole financial crisis was happening.

So this idea of connection and rhythm—that's all a part of driving culture. Culture isn't simply "Let's create a mission statement and that's our purpose." Culture is how you behave every day, and how you communicate, or *whether* you communicate, and what information you share and what information you don't share, and how you handle certain situations. That's all about driving culture.

Once you establish a good meeting rhythm, then you have to think about what the message should be in those meetings. Warner emphasizes that when you're communicating with your organization, everything you say and do should be tied back to the purpose of your mission:

I think to build connection with the organization, you need to always tie it back to purpose. So for us, we take care of patients, and everything we do ties back to that principle. I can tell you a little bit about how I changed my whole communication when I took over as CEO, because I really felt like I *wasn't* tying back to purpose prior to that. And I changed the whole way I communicated to make sure everything we did was tied back to purpose.

After I took over as CEO on September 1, 2012, about two weeks, three weeks into it, there was a big physician leadership meeting, and about one hundred doctors attended. And I had been thinking a lot about my plan for the next five years and what I wanted to do. I presented it to the physician leaders, and you know, nobody left, but it didn't really go over so well. Nobody was really inspired. And I talked about *US News* national rankings, and being the best, and growing and all that sort of thing. But a couple months later, I was having a conversation with our physician strategy cabinet about why people go into medicine. And why do people go into nursing? It's all about caring for people. And I remember taking a long walk to reflect, and I realized, "Yep, I missed the mark." It's all about tying everything we want to do back to patients and our purpose first.

So I came back, and I said, "We're going to change how we communicate during meetings. We're going to open every meeting with a patient story. We need to connect to purpose. And we need to take the message directly to the employees so that each and every one of them know they are critical to our success." So we started a quarterly event called The Power of One. Before these meetings, I think about the content that I'm writing, and we talk a lot about the theme, what I want to cover, what we want to accomplish, and we tie everything back to purpose. It gets back to, "Why does Ochsner exist? We exist to take care of patients." Ever since 2012, when we started those Power of One meetings, our engagement scores have improved every single year. Communicating our purpose paid off.

"If you are in a large organization, ask yourself what type of infrastructure or ecosystem you want to have around you in order to maximize your chances of success."

–JUAN MARTIN
GLOBAL PRESIDENT, KIND SNACKS AND NATURE'S BAKERY

I believe that your personal values drive your operational rhythm. It took me a while to discover and fully understand my three core values: trust, family, and curiosity. I probably had a pipeline of fifteen values that I liked that I thought were descriptive of me. But once I boiled them down to three, they completely changed the way I approach my interaction and connection with my organization. I would recommend every leader narrow down their value system to no more than three.

I'm always very mindful about how I allocate my personal time and business calendar. I try to follow a balanced approach: when one week gets more lopsided in one direction, then the following week needs to compensate in the other direction.

I prepare my agenda and interactions, particularly big town halls with thousands of people, based on my values. If you are in a large organization, start mapping out who your key stakeholders are. What type of infrastructure or ecosystem do you want to have around you to maximize your chances to be successful within the organization? And I don't mean career mapping or career planning. I mean figuring out what's the role of each element of your ecosystem to make the business successful.

The one thing I do to control my calendar, so that it doesn't control me, is that I plan a cadence of interactions that I want to have with each one of my stakeholders. For example, I speak to the founder of KIND every week, while I speak to the chairman of the board of Mars once a quarter. And that doesn't mean that one is more important than the other. But in order to create the infrastructure required for KIND to be successful, that's what I think is the right balance of interactions. And that balance can be a way to measure how you connect meaningfully with the critical stakeholders that will allow your organization to be successful.

"When brainstorming our meeting agendas, our ultimate goal is to develop our team into great hospitality leaders."

–ROBÉRT LEBLANC

FOUNDER, CEO, AND CREATIVE DIRECTOR, LEBLANC+SMITH

Robért LeBlanc believes in the importance of establishing a meeting rhythm.

My weekly meetings with my team are crucial. We have full team meetings with everybody in the company (about thirty to forty people) every Wednesday and Friday for fifteen minutes on Zoom. I open the meeting by reading the vision statement, values, and company goals.

We go through the performance really quickly from the previous week, and then we talk about a learning and development lesson. I'll pick something that I know will lead to their development. Sometimes we cover a five- or six-minute session on how to do a great social media post, or how to be an ambassador of the restaurant and spread the word to get people to visit in an authentic and natural way. We'll talk about how to do an accounting entry in QuickBooks; we'll talk about how we analyze profit and loss statements.

Because our ultimate goal is to develop our team into great hospitality leaders.

And the last thing that we do in the last five minutes is address problems that we need to solve, collectively or individually, and you can submit those ahead of time. We define it as "stucks," things we're stuck on. For those who cannot join the call due to scheduling or obligation conflicts, we record the meetings and share them via Zoom links, so everyone has access to the meetings that they miss. But if you keep it to fifteen minutes, everybody participates and everybody's attentive. Everybody knows that it's all high-value content if we are keeping it to fifteen minutes.

To truly connect with the employees, we also do monthly check-ins. And we spend time talking about how they are doing and reinforcing the good behaviors. We believe that leaders will always drive excellent performance far more consistently by acknowledging, reinforcing, and rewarding good behaviors. We then spend a few moments letting them know what they need to work on to improve. However, the largest part of these meetings is listening. We'll spend five, six, seven minutes asking, "Tell us what's going on. How are you feeling?"

HERE'S WHAT WE'VE LEARNED

The "operating rhythm" is the foundation of effective leadership, and the operating calendar drives the organization for the entire year. Rather than working in a stressful, reactive state of mind, leaders should plan a cadence of interactions that they want to have with each of their stakeholders. Then they should proactively schedule their meetings in a systematized manner that aligns with their organization's structure. This schedule or rhythm can serve to measure whether the leader is connected with the most important stakeholders of the organization.

REFLECTION AND ACTION

Now that you've learned how our leaders successfully owned their calendars, please answer the following questions:

1. Do you own your calendar, or does your calendar own you?

2. On a scale of one to ten, how effectively do you manage your calendar?

3. Do you embed time to eat lunch? Stretch? Prepare for the next meeting? Strategically think?

4. Does your meeting rhythm reflect the most important stakeholders and the time you should spend with them?

5. How could you tweak your meeting rhythm so that it's more effective?

CHAPTER 10

LEADERS RECKON WITH COVID-19

A s I was interviewing leaders to learn about their best practices for connection, COVID-19 became the topic of the nightly news. Within weeks, we were in the middle of a global pandemic and under lockdown orders. After spending the first few weeks feeling numb and confused, I started seeing the leaders who I had interviewed for this book all over social media. They were trying to connect with their people, their organizations, their communities. That's when I realized I needed to reach out to them to learn how they were connecting in a time of crisis.

One of the first chiefs I called asked me to conduct a pulse check with his leaders to find out what was working, what was not working, and how he could best support them while they were working via Zoom from home.

The following themes emerged:

1. Communicate, communicate, communicate. People need to hear from their leaders at least on a weekly basis, sometimes on a daily basis during a crisis. They need their leaders to

communicate updates, provide hope, and remain calm in the storm. They need to feel some sense of normalcy and comfort that they are in good hands.

2. Take the time to meaningfully connect with employees, not just on a professional level but on a personal level. Schedule one-on-one check-ins. Ask how they are doing, not just what they are accomplishing. Make sure your staff knows that you care about them personally. Demonstrate empathy for how difficult the situation is.

3. Show appreciation for how hard your people are working under stressful conditions. Write thank-you notes or make thank-you videos. If you have the financial resources, give bonuses or gift cards. Demonstrating recognition and appreciation in a time of crisis is vital.

I then reached out to some of the leaders who I had interviewed previously and asked for examples of how they connected with their employees, teams, and organizations during the global pandemic.

You'll hear from Warner Thomas, Judi Terzotis, Larry Closs, Pete November, Robért LeBlanc, and Todd Graves.

"Approach the situation calmly and with confidence. Trust your experience and your belief that you will figure it out, and believe in your team."

—WARNER THOMAS
CEO, OCHSNER HEALTH

N ew Orleans was one of the initial epicenters of the coronavirus outbreak. On March 11, 2020, Ochsner admitted its first COVID-19 patient. That number jumped to nine hundred patients in just twenty-two days.

When asked about his leadership style during COVID-19, CEO Warner Thomas said:

> I think part of it is giving license to my team to run with it. Giving people clarity by saying, "Look, go take this project on, or go open these testing sites, open these ICU beds," or whatever it is. "Manage the issues, the challenges, or problems that you'll run into; you got license to do it." But I think there's two sides to that. There's feeling like you're empowered to do it, and then taking the initiative yourself and not putting self-limiting behaviors on it.
>
> I've learned that I'm a lot more calm and a lot more collected than I had been previously, and I chalk a lot of that up to experience and improved self-confidence. I chalk it up to the belief that we will figure it out, and I believe in my team. Because when you've gone through a few very difficult times, you know you just have to figure it out.
>
> I think what I've tried to do differently during this crisis is to push a lot more messages directly to employees. In the beginning I was doing a weekly brief of, "Okay, here's where we are, here's what we know." And I think people needed that.

> "If your organization is medium-sized, write a personal note to staff members thanking them for their patience through the crisis, and ask if they need any additional support. Try to personally touch as many people as possible."

–JUDI TERZOTIS

PUBLISHER AND PRESIDENT, THE *TIMES-PICAYUNE* | *THE ADVOCATE*

Judi Terzotis discussed the importance of reaching out to her staff one on one with daily check-ins:

My leadership style has always been very hands-on, but I felt like I had to really ratchet it up. So in my daily routine, I would try to pick out two or three employees and send them a personal note saying either "Hey, I'm checking in on you. How are you doing?" or "I noticed that you've been working some really long hours. Is there anything I can do for you?"

I pulled a payroll list. I just went through it and said, "Okay, who haven't I reached yet?" I've surprised some folks who I don't necessarily interact with on a given day in normal circumstances, which is good.

It started with the mindset of "Who are the people that are really on the frontline, and who are the ones that are under a lot of pressure?" And I swept that group, and I've gone back to a few of them again because I just know they're burning the candle at both ends. I'm trying to circle the horn, if you will, to feel like I personally have touched as many people as possible.

Judi instituted nightly emails, calls, and virtual town hall meetings to maintain connection with her organization.

When [COVID-19] started to bubble up, we immediately started an evening update email. I asked my leadership team to give me some submissions, and I tried to write it so that the staff realized, "Hey, it's tough right now, but we've got this. And here are some things that are happening because you physically aren't in the same space right now." So I wanted to make sure that they knew that business is moving forward, and it wasn't at a screeching halt.

So I did that Monday through Thursday every night. On Fridays, we already had a weekly newsletter, so I let that newsletter kind of speak as the recap for the week. But I've gotten feedback about how important it is to our staff to hear from me every day. When you communicate, you want to communicate for a reason, not just to communicate. So that is a tactic that has worked.

WHEN YOU COMMUNICATE, YOU WANT TO COMMUNICATE FOR A REASON, NOT JUST TO COMMUNICATE.

We've conducted many virtual town hall meetings. During the first town hall, which we did via Zoom, the staff asked very tough questions anonymously. For the next town hall, I asked the staff what's on their minds beforehand, so I could prepare better to answer their questions.

We've done a good job with a nightly executive Zoom call. And we talk about the day, and part of the conversation is "Oh, so-and-so just really went out of his way. You wouldn't believe what goes into putting on a live town hall. I really would appreciate it if you all would reach out to him and thank him." And that happens organically; it's not just coming from the department head.

"Acknowledge to your staff that there are some dangers out there. But try to keep things as normal as possible while being cognizant of those dangers."

–LARRY CLOSS

CEO, MAXHOME

So this news about COVID-19 was coming at me in slow dribs and drabs as the leader, but it was very important to get way out in front of that. There are three parts to messaging:

1. There's the message.

2. There's the tone.

3. There's the manner.

The tone in my case was always, for lack of a better word, familiar. I made it family-like, which I think was crucial. I mean, treat the company as you would a family.

So the family tone, which was not faked, was "I care about you; these are the things that we need to do to be safe." I was cognizant very early on in this, and especially in February and March, that something was going to happen. And I had to make sure that I had that tone of safety.

But I have to tell you, there was an internal split in people, a split in what people cared about. Whether they thought about safety, or whether they thought about their jobs. Some people thought coronavirus was BS or that it wasn't a big deal, while other people were scared to death of it. "What about my job? How am I going to pay my bills? How am I going to live? Am I going to be homeless? Are you going to lay me off?" And there were a lot of moving parts to figure out how to deal with that. But in those communications, we just had to normalize things as much as possible. No different than you would with the kids in the family, right? "Hey, there's some dangers out there. But let's try to keep things as normal as possible while being cognizant of those dangers."

We moved virtually before a lot of other people did because we saw some danger in bringing people together. So I started jumping into Zoom meetings. I used to send handwritten notes of appreciation, but I switched all of that to videos during the crisis. I probably sent three videos a day to people thanking them. Plus I made a point of personally talking to every manager every week in the early stages.

And then we upped our executive communication to once a day instead of once a week. But this was all a very fluid thing. The once-a-day executive meetings probably happened for two weeks, and then we would say, "Okay, everyone has to keep this time in their calendar open, and we will just call it if we need it." But I think one of the keys to communication during this crisis was not only harping on safety but also just keeping everybody informed on all of the different things happening as cities were closing down.

"Not micromanaging during a crisis is really important. You've got to hire really good people and trust them to do their jobs and support them in that effort."

−PETE NOVEMBER

EXECUTIVE VICE PRESIDENT AND CHIEF FINANCIAL OFFICER, OCHSNER HEALTH

When discussing best practices of leading during a crisis, specifically the COVID-19 crisis, Pete said that the team should feel secure and supported, and that managers should assume positive intent:

First, during a crisis, I think everyone needs to know that they are supported 110 percent, not only supported in terms of what they get done but supported as individuals and humans. And I use the words *loved* and *supported*. Because I think when staff feel that they are loved and supported, they can excel because they're comfortable.

In addition, I've learned in my role that human beings assume the worst. Instead, we all have to assume positive intent and seek to understand why people are doing what they're doing. And I think it takes effort, and I think you have to train yourself to assume positive intent. It doesn't come automatically. Because most of the time there's no ill intent. It's just that they have a reason why they're acting a certain way. And once you understand that, then you can relate to them and figure out how to solve it. But I don't think people often take the time to really understand why people are conducting themselves in a certain way, especially during a stressful time like a quarantine.

Not micromanaging is really important. You've got to hire really good people and trust them to do their jobs and support them. Think of yourself like a parent. You've got to trust them. And I think one of the things we learned in the crisis is that there's so much that you have to deal with, you have to give people the freedom to run, and you just have to trust them. And when you do that, they excel.

When I asked Pete how he was able to build a team that he trusts in the first place, he said:

Well, first it was a lot of time spent trying to get them to build relationships with one another and to trust each other. And to trust that I had their back. Some of my leaders came into working with me from a place where they didn't always feel trusted and supported.

And so we did a lot of forcing them to build relationships with one another. Well, not really "force" but making it such a priority that they had no choice but to just develop the relationships. I told them to talk to one another and figure it out, as opposed to making me figure it out *for* them.

Pete discussed how his organization faced the unprecedented challenge of COVID-19 head on:

I think it goes back to when the fire hit, we had a choice. We could have chosen *not* to face it head on, we could have chosen not to support our people, we could have gotten upset because of all the financial and uncertainty we were facing. But instead we said, "We're going to support our people 100 percent. We're going to be innovative. We're going to face this challenge, and we're going to do it together." And a lot of people looked at us like we were crazy. I remember someone called me when we were three days into it and asked, "What do you think about all the talk about cutting staff?" I said, "We're not doing that. We spent all this time talking about how much we care for our people, and the minute it gets tough, we are going to start cutting our people?" He said, "I totally agree, but I just had to ask because there's people that think the other way." And I said, "Yeah, we're not doing that." Our CEO was relentless about caring for our people and our patients first, and that focus radiated throughout the organization and gave us the foundation to succeed.

"Daily meetings kept us connected during a very stressful time and gave us purpose and a clear vision. While it has been challenging, it's also been really inspiring. People are learning so much, and they are so much more engaged than they ever were before."

—ROBÉRT LEBLANC
FOUNDER, CEO, AND CREATIVE DIRECTOR, LEBLANC+SMITH

---

made a decision to close down on March 15, which was four days before the city mandate. We had to let everybody go, which was excruciating. I'm not one who gets depressed, but I was feeling like a huge failure. But we developed a standard operating procedure on the best and most efficient way to be available and on call for our people. And every day at three o'clock, even though we didn't have anything to cover, we'd have a meeting with our five leaders. There was no business to discuss. So in the beginning we went around and just checked in: "Tell me how you're feeling, what you're going through; tell me if there's anything you've learned that you think the rest of us should know." These meetings kept us connected during a very stressful time. More importantly, they began to give us purpose and a clear vision on how we could return and get as many people back to work as safely as possible.

Before COVID-19, I'd been studying stoic philosophy for about a year and a half. The premise of stoic philosophy is "We cannot control the things that happen to us. We can only control how we respond." And so eventually I realized maybe this means we have an opportunity to reinvent the hospitality model that's been broken for so long. A business model that has broken so many lives.

I read about Toyota's "lean" manufacturing system. Lean is based on seeing and eliminating waste and the process of continuous improvement. So we asked ourselves, How can we survive with half the sales? We would probably have to survive with half the people. And given all the challenges in life, we'd have to pay them more. And so we studied the idea of lean manufacturing and Pareto's Principle, which means that 20 percent of the work that you do produces 80 percent of the outcomes. And we looked at all the things that we were doing, and we realized how much we did that was wasteful, redundant, and not important to accomplishing our goal, which is to create excellent, inspiring, and fulfilling experiences for our guests and for our team so that they can become great hospitality leaders.

So after seeing all the waste and eliminating it, then you work on the process of continuous improvement. You think about everything in the context of "How can we be more efficient and more effective with our time?"

For example, we break down all the responsibilities of the business into annually, quarterly, monthly, weekly, and daily, and every responsibility has a process attached to it. And so during COVID-19, I looked at the system that we have. We have the written processes in Google Drive, which shows you how to do everything. But it's really, really detailed, about 150 processes and 278 responsibilities. So we said, "Let's talk about being lean. And let's say we have less than half the people when we reopen. What do we have to eliminate, or what has to go?" What are the most important things?

So we cut it down to thirty-two processes and seventy-eight responsibilities. It became much simpler.

Our business model before COVID-19 was comprised entirely of specialists, and we went back to the idea of being generalists after COVID-19. There are times when the chef works the host stand and checks guests in or takes orders at tables. Everybody washes dishes. Certain things require a little bit more skill and experience, so not everybody can fully do everything. But we include the entire team in all the decisions. We used to have management meetings with just the general manager, the chef, and the bartender, but now our meetings include everybody. And we call them "open source, open content." We talk freely about how we're performing financially; we talk honestly and openly about how we're thinking about decisions. And everyone has got a voice and has a say or a vote in the outcomes. So while it has been challenging, because COVID-19 is just such a weird, unpredictable time, it's been really inspiring. People are learning so much, and they are so much more engaged than they ever were before.

"Leaders should know that in crisis situations, you must act quickly. There isn't time to spend days planning a call or working on agendas."

–TODD GRAVES

FOUNDER AND CEO, RAISING CANE'S

When speaking about the COVID-19 pandemic, Todd felt that because his team had persevered through serious situations before, they were prepared for the worst:

My co-CEO AJ Kumaran and I started tracking COVID-19 early on in the process. Hurricane Katrina taught me a lot, but the most important thing I learned is to fully expect the unexpected. Expect the worst, plan for it, and then hope for the best. Because that's what happened after Katrina. We were used to hurricanes; we had a hurricane plan, but we could have never dreamed the levees would break. When that happened, I realized we needed a whole other plan. So we began following the COVID-19 crisis in China and tracked it as it made its way to the US.

Restaurants make small margins on very large volumes. When you are a restaurant owner and your cash flow stops, your first concern is "Can I keep my team employed?" When you're a small business, this is a major concern and can potentially shut your doors. Because we have a large credit line, I wasn't worried about that. However, I feared that I may have to let some of my crew go. I did *not* want that to happen, so we started making plans and working with our banks to secure our credit lines. We informed our managers that we were monitoring the situation, and while we didn't know a lot about it, we were tracking it.

Todd discussed keeping his crew continuously informed of the ongoing developments during the crisis:

When COVID-19 came to the US, we knew clear and constant communication with our crew was key. So we set up our messaging—a general message for crew members working in the restaurants and a more detailed message to our restaurant leaders and restaurant support office. For our crew, we started with very basic information about COVID-19, how it's very contagious. We said to them, "You have to take care of yourself, cover your cough and sneezes, don't get around people you think may be sick. If you have any symptoms like fever, chills, cough, don't come to work." Once we learned more, and the CDC released info, we communicated that. These were short one-minute videos educating them on how to protect themselves, each other, and our customers as well as what to do if they became sick.

We communicated via video because we believe it's important for our crew to see me and AJ talking to them, knowing we were here to support them. With today's technology, it's so easy to make a quick video on my phone and quickly get it to our crew. When it's real time and organic like that, it often resonates with our crew more. There are times when we have a film crew and teleprompters when we need more produced content; however, we needed to communicate quickly, and our organic approach worked.

We'd have weekly calls keeping everyone updated, as well as impromptu calls when something would come up that we wanted to address. Leaders should know that in these situations, you must act quickly. There isn't time to spend days planning a call, working on agendas, etc. You have to quickly gather your thoughts and get everybody on a call.

Todd spoke about the decision to reopen as an "essential business" during the pandemic, and how he helped to rally the restaurant crew to come together during such a difficult time:

I rallied everybody around the idea that we needed to reopen for three really big reasons:

1. We needed a place for our crew to come back to work. We needed cash flow to keep everyone employed.

2. We needed to be there for our customers and to come back for the community. Not only were we feeding frontline workers, but with many restaurants closed, our communities needed a safe place to eat.

3. If Raising Cane's was going to survive, we needed to rally together. When you have a unified purpose, everyone can get behind it. I believe that in times of crisis, leaders emerge, teams are formed, and people pull through. I think it's the leader's job to rally people around a really meaningful cause.

At the beginning of COVID-19, our sales were down 30 percent because dine-in and takeout were shut down, and we were bleeding cash. Our mantra became "No crew left behind." I wanted to make sure that the team that we went into this pandemic with was the same team we were going to come out with. "We're going to work, and we're going to fight like hell so no one loses their job." Our crew was so strong; everyone worked so hard, so diligently, and they worked well together. We had a shared purpose—and it's amazing what happens when you have a shared purpose.

IT'S AMAZING WHAT HAPPENS WHEN YOU HAVE A SHARED PURPOSE.

We went from being 30 percent down to reaching our forecasted sales to now doing more than we originally projected. It's just really incredible, and I couldn't be prouder of my crew. I believe our crew feels like "We're part of the solution too. Todd says we're going in, and no one's losing their job. But we all got to fight like hell to make sure that happens."

We printed gold- and silver-foiled keepsake documents stating that they were essential workers. We designed keepsake pins that they can wear on their hats that read "COVID-19 Response Team." We gave them "No Crew Left Behind" stickers and created signs for the restaurant. To show our appreciation for their extraordinary work, we then distributed $5 million in "thank-you" bonuses system-wide after our sales rebounded.

HERE'S WHAT WE'VE LEARNED

During a crisis, leaders need to:

- Approach the crisis calmly and with confidence, trusting their experience and believing in their teams.

- Act quickly. There isn't time to spend days planning a call or working on agendas.

- Provide clear and constant communication, at least on a weekly basis, sometimes on a daily basis.

- Offer hope and remain calm in the storm.

- Acknowledge that there are some dangers, but also keep routines as normal as possible.

- Take the time to meaningfully connect with each employee, not just on a professional level but on a personal level.

- Demonstrate empathy and understanding for how difficult the situation can be during a crisis.

- Recognize and show appreciation for how hard everyone is working despite the stressful conditions.

REFLECTION AND ACTION

Think about how you handled the COVID-19 crisis or another business crisis. Please reflect and answer the following questions:

1. Once the crisis occurred, how often did you communicate with your employees?

2. How did you meaningfully connect with each person on your team?

3. What would you do differently?

4. Did you have the right technology to pivot during the crisis?

5. What lessons outlined in the chapter can you apply to your organization?

CONCLUSION

A seismic shift in leadership has occurred. Leaders who rely on the old characteristics of power, control, and fear are becoming more and more ineffective. We are in a new era: an era that demands connection. The next generation of leaders will create cultures of connection instead of cultures of fear.

WE ARE IN A NEW ERA: AN ERA THAT DEMANDS CONNECTION.

Authenticity, compassion, and alignment are the foundations for meaningful connection. You've learned strategies for how to connect with yourself including owning your story, giving up the quest for perfection, and owning your communication style.

You've learned strategies for how to connect with your employees including showing care and compassion for the whole person, listening to lead, and acting as a servant leader.

You've learned strategies for how to connect to your organization including aligning your values with the company's values, creating a positive culture, and owning your calendar. And finally, you learned effective strategies for how to connect in a crisis.

Through my years as a leadership coach and business professor, I've observed that if you're going to be the best version of yourself, whether you're the coach of a sports team, a nonprofit executive, or the president of your family's business, whether leading a small organization or a Fortune 500 company, **the secret sauce lies in your ability to connect**.

As Matthew Lieberman says, "Connection is a superpower that makes human beings smarter, happier, and more productive."[33]

I want you to create environments where you show care and compassion for yourself and those you work with. Where you invest the time to develop healthy relationships. Where you value authenticity over perfection. Where your teams are motivated to collaborate, cooperate, and work together toward a common goal.

Now go forth and connect.

---

33   Michael Stallard, "Seven Practices That Protect Your Organization from the Lethality of Loneliness," *Forbes*, June 18, 2018, https://
www.forbes.com/sites/forbescoachescouncil/2018/06/18/
seven-practices-that-protect-your-organization-from-the-lethality-of-loneliness/.

AFTERWORD

On a swampy August afternoon, as the sputtering window unit in my apartment struggled to blow cold air, I pressed the phone close to my ear so that I could hear Dr. Johnston speak over the grumbling thunder outside. "Well," she said, "why don't you tell me what you've learned during this process?"

I drew in my breath. I had been working with Dr. Johnston for a year as her graduate assistant, learning about connection and communication from her while participating in various projects for her management classes. For the past three months, we had labored on my biggest assignment yet, assisting her with the creation of her very first book on leadership. We had just put the finishing touches on the rough draft of her manuscript and were discussing how I felt about the experience. I was relieved and enthusiastic at the same time, thankful that the project had been completed and excited about what would come next.

I reflected inwardly on the previous months' work, startled by what I discovered about myself during the book-writing process. Oftentimes, I had wondered if Dr. Johnston was speaking directly to me through her passages.

I struggled with the concept of authenticity through much of my adult life. My peaceful childhood turned tragic when my mother was diagnosed with Lou Gehrig's disease, an incurable and fatal neurological disorder. I was only fourteen years old at the time and was naturally terrified at the idea of losing my mom. Unable to cope with my growing anxiety, I lashed out. I started skipping school, and my grades fell drastically. I ran with a wild crowd and caused plenty of trouble. I ended up dropping out of high school, opting to receive my GED instead at seventeen years old. By then, I was needed at home to care for my mother (who was in a wheelchair by this time) and for my younger brother, who was experiencing many of the same issues that I did. My relationship with my mother had blossomed into a beautiful friendship when she died at the age of forty-six. I was twenty-two years old at the time of her funeral.

I didn't know what to do with myself after that. If I had known better, I would've sought grief counseling right away. But instead I buried that trauma deep inside myself. I didn't discuss what I had experienced with anyone, embarrassed that my past was so different from those around me. My coworkers never knew anything about it; I very carefully selected the persona that I wanted the world to see. I continued to lash out but in different ways. My relationships suffered greatly, and I lost many friends because I had difficulty showing compassion and empathy. I found it impossible to stick to commitments. I felt split in half as though I had two identities: the inauthentic, fake, extra tough version of me that I showed to the world, and the real me who was floundering inside. I didn't know how to behave or how to fix myself.

I decided to start taking classes at the local community college where I immediately rediscovered my love of learning. My grades were high, and I was elated to transfer into the university system two years later. There, I earned my bachelor's degree and began applying for professional jobs. But while employers were eager to grant me a first interview, many times I would receive a call back saying that another candidate had been selected to fill the position. In fact, there were two separate times when I passed through three rounds of phone and in-person interviews, only to be rejected for the job at the final moments. I couldn't figure out what I was doing wrong.

Meanwhile, my younger brother happily rebounded from his own personal difficulties. He followed the same path that I did, entering the university by way of community college, and I had never been prouder of him. Only my brother acted in a completely different way than I did. Instead of hiding that he was a returning adult student, he was open and forthcoming about it. He sought therapy for his grief. He didn't hide his past from his peers, instead using the trauma that we experienced to foster deep, genuine connections with others. He made friends easily and was well liked by all his classmates. His college within the university gave him the privilege of carrying their banner at the graduation ceremony, and his story of perseverance received a front-page write-up in our city's newspaper.

Not only that, but my brother edged out over two hundred applicants for a highly coveted marketing internship at a storied insurance company. In his application essay, he discussed our family's history to demonstrate his skills of resilience, drive, and determination. In just a few short years, he has already received a promotion and has moved into a beautiful home with his wife and five pets.

"Even though my brother's successes were staring me in the face, it didn't occur to me that being inauthentic was hindering my ability to move forward in life, both personally and in my professional career," I told Dr. Johnston. "Of course employers felt like I was being fake during my interviews—I *was* being fake!" I laughed. "I have learned so much through this process. Everything from how I dress to how I style my hair, the words that I use when speaking to others, it's all been so meticulously crafted to conform to what *I think* the other person wants to see and hear! And only through the creation of this manuscript have I realized how much I have been sabotaging myself this entire time.

"Certainly everyone has experienced some amount of trauma, but the way I've persevered against all odds is what makes me unique among others," I said thoughtfully. I paused before saying aloud: "*The things that make me unique are the things that I need to show to the world.* They comprise my 'unique value proposition' in marketing speak," I laughed.

"I think you're finally owning your story, and that's the first step to truly connecting with yourself," said Dr. Johnston.

"I'm living proof of the truthfulness of your research," I replied. "It goes so far beyond connection within the business world. You've provided me with the tools to embrace my past instead of being embarrassed by it. To instead view it as what makes me special ... to give myself permission to become one whole person again."

A bolt of lightning lit up the sky as we ended our phone call. I wiped a tear from my eye and contemplated my next steps forward.

—Christina M. Jackson
August 2020